The Four-Blocks®
Literacy Model

Writing Mini-Lessons for First Grade:
The Four-Blocks® Model

by
Dorothy P. Hall,
Patricia M. Cunningham,
and Denise B. Boger

Carson-Dellosa Publishing Company, Inc.
Greensboro, North Carolina

Credits

Editor:
Joey Bland

Cover Design:
Dez Perrotti

Layout Design:
Joey Bland

Artist:
Julie Kinlaw

Printed in the USA • All rights reserved   ISBN 0-88724-813-6

Dedication

This book is dedicated to:

My three daughters—**Angelyn**, **Amie**, and **Allie**.

Denise Boger

Margaret Defee, who taught the three of us about thinking aloud and writing for children and whose lessons, like Denise's, we tried to capture in this book.

Pat Cunningham, Dottie Hall, and Denise Boger

Table of Contents

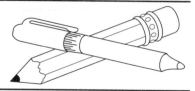

Table of Contents

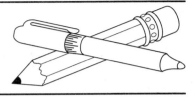

Introduction

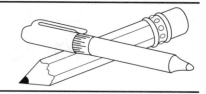

Writing Mini-Lessons for First Grade

Writing is a critical part of a balanced literacy program for first-graders. Some children have been read to since birth and have learned to write in kindergarten; others have not. In every first grade class there are students who have not had many experiences with books and print. Imagine how strange the funny black marks on a page must look to children who have not had much experience with books. Have you ever looked at something written in Arabic or Chinese and wondered how anyone could ever make sense of it? To many first graders, the little black marks that are our English words make as little sense as the writing in nonalphabetic systems makes to us.

In first grade, the most basic concept that children must grasp is that writing is "talk written down." The black marks are not foreign, indecipherable symbols. The black marks are our words—the same words that we say. During writing time each day in first grade, we show children the very essence of what reading and writing are. We invite children to enter the abstract world of reading and writing through the very real world of their daily lives.

For many first-graders, writing is their easiest route to learning to read. If you observed the writing time in a first-grade classroom each day and saw the teacher writing in front of the children and then encouraging the children in their writing, it would be natural to think that the major goal of this writing time was to teach children to write. Early in the year, however, the major goal of the writing time is not to teach writing, but rather to use writing as a way to launch children into successful reading. As the year goes on and more children become readers, the writing time does indeed become a time when the major goal is to teach children how to write.

The distinction between viewing writing as a child-centered personal approach to reading and viewing writing as a way to produce better writers is critical to the success of the writing time early in first grade. If you see writing as a way to teach reading, you won't worry when you can't read what the students wrote! As long as your students are thinking of what they want to say and using whatever letter-sound and word skills they have at that point to represent their ideas, then you have a successful "writing approach to reading" operating in your classroom.

If you think that a writing approach to reading sounds a little strange and unusual, consider what happens with many four- and five-year-olds before they ever come to school. Have you ever observed young children taking a piece of notebook paper and "doing homework" like their big brothers or sisters by copying words on the paper? Have you noticed that the first words many young children can read are words they can also write? Many four-year-olds have a personal reading vocabulary of important-to-them words, which include their names; the names of their brothers, sisters, and pets; a favorite restaurant; and an important phrase or two. They often write these words in all capital letters and sometimes mix up the order of some of the letters.

DAVID   MAMA   DADDY   BAER   PIZZA HUT   I LOVE YUO   KEEP OUT

Preschool children like to draw and often add words, letters, and numbers to their drawings. Children get these words by asking adults to spell them for them and by copying them from various print around the house.

If you think about your own experiences with four- and five-year-old children, you will realize that combining words, letters, and numbers along with drawings is a very natural activity. These "lucky" children whose early writing efforts have been encouraged, applauded, and often displayed with pride on the refrigerator rarely have trouble learning to read when they come to school. Regardless of what approach to teaching reading they encounter in first grade, they have already been successfully launched into reading through a very natural writing approach to reading.

Reading and Writing in Four-Blocks First Grades

In Four-Blocks first grades, we devote 30 to 40 minutes each day to each of the major approaches to learning to read. (For more information about Four-Blocks, see *The Teacher's Guide to the Four-Blocks®* by Cunningham, Hall and Sigmon.) During the Self-Selected Reading Block, the teacher reads aloud to the children and then the children read books of their own choosing. While the children read, the teacher has individual conferences with them about their self-selected books. (For more information on Self-Selected Reading, see *Self-Selected Reading the Four-Blocks® Way* by Cunningham, Hall, and Gambrell.) During the Guided Reading Block, we focus on comprehension, language, and concept development as we guide the children reading in a variety of different kinds of texts. (For more information on Guided Reading see *Guided Reading the Four-Blocks® Way* by Cunningham, Hall, and Cunningham.) During the Working with Words Block, we teach children how to read and spell high-frequency words and the letter-sound patterns needed to decode and spell other words. Four-Blocks classrooms use a variety of before and after reading activities to teach comprehension skills and strategies. Teachers are encouraged to use a variety of during reading formats also. (For more information on Working with Words, see *Month-by-Month Phonics for First Grade* by Cunningham and Hall.) During the Writing Block, children write and share each day, and they observe the teacher writing and thinking about writing during the daily writing mini-lesson. The Writing Block serves a dual function. Children who have limited literacy skills have the opportunity to use writing as an approach to learning to read. As the year goes on and children develop some reading skills, the focus of the Writing Block shifts to helping children become better writers.

The mini-lesson is critical to the success of the Writing Block, and the focus of the mini-lessons changes as we proceed through the first-grade year. We have divided the mini-lessons in this book into three sections: Mini-Lessons for Early in First Grade, Mini-Lessons for Most of First Grade, and Mini-Lessons for Late in First Grade. How many lessons you do and how many times you do a mini-lesson depends upon your students and their abilities.

Mini-Lessons for Early in First Grade—Getting Started

Early in first grade, we are using writing as an approach to reading. We emphasize writing as putting down on paper "what you want to tell." We think aloud about what we want to "tell" the students and we tell them by drawing and writing a few words during the mini-lesson. As the children write, we circulate around the room and "encourage" the children. We don't spell words for them, but we help them stretch out words and we point them to places in the room where they can find the correct spellings of words. After 10 to 15 minutes of drawing and writing time, we bring the children together and have them "tell" about what they were drawing and writing. One question we are constantly asked is, "How long is spent using the early-in-the-year focus on writing as an approach to reading?" That is a question you will have to answer for yourself, and the answer you come up with this year will not necessarily be the right answer for next year. First-graders vary greatly in their entering literacy knowledge. In some schools, many children come to first grade knowing how to make most of the letters, as well as knowing how to read and write some words. These children have usually experienced the writing-approach-to-reading either at home or in kindergarten. They know what those "little black marks" are, and they know that reading is just translating those marks into words they can say. They come to first grade already reading and writing a little, and the writing time can soon become a time to focus primarily on learning to write better. Unfortunately, many first-graders have not had these early writing experiences at home or in kindergarten, and they need a longer period of time where the emphasis is on what they want to tell and not on how well they write. Here are some of the signs to look for to let you know when you can place a greater emphasis on helping children become better writers.

Most days, most students in the class:

- seem comfortable using words and pictures to put down what they want to tell.
- use the Word Wall and other print displays in the room to spell words.
- stretch out unknown words that are not available in the room, getting down enough letters so that most words are decipherable.
- can write one or more sentences that they can read back to us.
- can tell about what they have drawn and written during the daily circle time.

Once most of the children display these behaviors **most** of the time, we can move on.

Mini-Lessons for Most of First Grade—Continuing to Learn

As the first-grade year continues, the writing time begins to look more like a Writer's Workshop and more like it does at other grade levels. The Author's Chair procedures are established. One-fifth of the children are designated to share writing each day. They read one piece they have written since their last sharing day, then they call on other students to tell something they liked about the piece and to ask questions. The teacher also establishes the publishing procedures. In most classrooms, children pick one piece to publish when they have three good pieces written. The teacher's time, which previously had been spent circulating and encouraging children in their writing, is now allocated primarily to writing conferences in which she helps the children revise, edit, and publish their pieces.

What type of paper the children write on usually changes, too. Early in the year, children usually draw and write on unlined drawing paper or on half-and-half paper and drawing is included with the writing each day. Once Author's Chair and publishing begins, drawing is not usually included each day, although many teachers let the children draw a picture to go with the piece of writing they plan to share in the Author's Chair. Of course, illustrations are also drawn to go with published books. Most teachers establish writing folders or writing notebooks for children, and the children keep all of their first-draft writing in these notebooks or folders.

Editing and learning to use an Editor's Checklist are important components of how children learn to become better writers. An Editor's Checklist begins with an item or two, and the children edit the teacher's writing each day for the items on the checklist. Before putting away their writing each day, the students are asked to do a quick edit of their own writing for the items on the checklist. Items on the checklist are added gradually with the teacher taking cues from the children's ability to edit for the items already on the list before adding other items. Once publishing begins, all children are not writing first drafts during the writing time each day. Some children are working to produce the three good pieces that will allow them to pick one to publish. Other children are conferencing with the teacher and preparing to publish. Other children are copying (or typing) and illustrating their published pieces.

Mini-Lessons for Later in First Grade—Getting Better

Depending on how your children are progressing and how long you needed to spend on "early-in-first-grade" procedures, you may be able to focus on more sophisticated writing strategies late in the year. We do mini-lessons in which we teach some simple revision strategies and then teach the children to partner edit. For most of first grade, we encourage the children to write about whatever topics they choose, in whatever form they choose. Late in the year, however, some focused writing weeks should be included in which to teach the children how to write particular forms and on particular topics. Often, this focused writing is compiled into class books or take-home books that students can read over and over again during the summer.

The Mini-Lessons

Doing a good mini-lesson every day is critical to the success of the Writing Block. The mini-lesson is your chance to show your children how to do all the different things writers do. We keep the mini-lesson brief—8 to 10 minutes—and do some writing or work with a piece of writing every day. A mini-lesson usually focuses on one skill or strategy that we need to teach or reteach the students. As we write, and before and after writing, we "think aloud" about what we are doing. This allows the children to see how to make all the decisions a writer must make. For example, we think aloud about what to write and how to write it:

"Let's see. What do I want to tell you today? I could tell you about what I did during our snow day yesterday, or I could tell you about my best friend when I was in first grade. I know! I will make a list of the places I would like to go on vacation."

We think aloud about different spelling strategies:

"I can look up on the Word Wall to spell **friends** because we just put it up there last week. I can stretch out vacation—**va-ca-shun**. I can spell **North Carolina** because it is on the map. I can spell **tent** because I know it rhymes with the Word Wall word **went**.

We think aloud about punctuation and capital letters:

"This ends my sentence, and since it is an exciting sentence, I will put an exclamation mark. I start my next sentence with a capital **D. Kristen** needs a capital **K** because it is someone's name."

We think aloud about revision and adding on:

"This is the piece I began yesterday and didn't have time to finish. I will reread what I wrote yesterday to get my brain thinking again. I am going to change **wet** to **soaked** because I was really soaked when I got home. Now, I can tell you where I finally found my dog."

We do many different mini-lessons focused on the same writing strategy. We return to strategies we previously taught whenever we observe in the children's writing something they particularly need to focus on.

Once we begin using an Editor's Checklist, we have the children do a quick check of our writing each day for the items on the list. When we start modeling how to add on to a piece and write a piece across several days, we wait until we have finished the piece and then use the whole day's mini-lesson to have the class edit the entire piece for the items on the list.

We also do mini-lessons on how to select a piece to publish. On these days, the children are not watching us write; they are watching us look at and think aloud about which of several pieces we most want to publish. Once we have chosen a piece to publish, we do a mini-lesson in which the children help us do some simple revisions and then we re-edit the entire piece. We then do mini-lessons in which we show the students how we turn an edited piece into a published book. The students watch us go through the stages of deciding how much to put on each page, carefully copying or typing the pages, illustrating the pages, and assembling the book.

Because it is impossible to know how many mini-lessons you will need for each focus, this book includes one full mini-lesson for each topic and then possibilities for other lessons. These other lessons can be done immediately after the first one, or you can return to a focus weeks later when your observations of your children's writing let you know that they need review and reteaching.

Over the years, we have observed that teachers who have the most successful writers in their classrooms faithfully do a daily mini-lesson in which they model and think-aloud about every aspect of the writing process. In fact, we have concluded that the quality, variety, and explicitness of the mini-lessons usually distinguishes teachers who enjoy the Writing Block from those who don't. We have tried in this book to capture the spirit and essence of all the excellent first-grade mini-lessons we have seen and to share this with you so that you and your children can feel happier and more successful with writing.

Early in First Grade—Getting Started

Early in first grade, we are using writing as an approach to reading. We emphasize writing as putting down on paper "what you want to tell." For our first mini-lessons, we put a large piece of unlined paper on the board and we talk as we draw a simple picture. We write a few words—labels, names, or a simple sentence. We do all our drawing and writing with markers and model the drawing and writing that many pre-schoolers do, referred to it as "driting." Next, we give the children large pieces of drawing paper and ask them to use their crayons to draw and write what they want to tell us. As they draw and write, we circulate around the room and "encourage" them. We respond to what they are drawing and ask them to tell us about it. We don't spell words for them but we help them stretch out words and we point them to places in the room where they can find the correct spellings of words. After 10 to 15 minutes of drawing and writing time, we bring the children together in a circle and have them "tell" what they are drawing and writing about.

When most children start including some words with their drawings and begin to catch on to how to use words in the room and stretch out words, we shift the kind of paper the children write on to "half-and-half" paper, with writing lines at the bottom and drawing space at the top. Many teachers create half-and-half transparencies or write on chart paper with writing lines and picture space. Now, we write a sentence or two first, using a black marker. Then, we switch to colored markers and draw our picture. We give the children half-and-half paper and ask them to write at least one sentence with their pencils before they draw with their crayons.

As the children begin to write, we provide one-on-one help to our most struggling children. We ask them to whisper a sentence to us or we ask them what they want to tell and then help them construct a simple sentence or two. We then help them stretch out the words in their sentences and point them to words on the Word Wall and on other print displays. We help them put a "finger space" between words and we ask them to read their sentence back to us, pointing to each word as they read. This individual daily coaching of our most struggling writers makes a remarkable difference in their abilities to get a sentence written that they can read and talk about.

We also pay some attention to our advanced writers, reading what they have written with them, and marveling at how well they used the print resources in the room and stretched out words to write three whole sentences! Writing in the "half-and-half" stage is very multilevel. With your help, all children can get a sentence written, and the paper has plenty of room for three or four sentences. When you gather the children in a circle for sharing, be sure to comment on all "the interesting things they thought of to tell," and "their spectacular drawings—much better than mine," as well as on how much and how well they have written. They will all feel successful if you brag on their ideas, drawings, and writing!

On the following pages are some of the mini-lessons we do early in first grade. We do as many of each as our particular class needs. We come back to lessons done earlier if we notice children who need to have that strategy reviewed. If you notice something that your children need to focus on during the driting and half-and-half stages that is not covered in these mini-lessons, create some mini-lessons of your own using the lessons outlined here as models. (Send the ideas to us if you like, and we will be eternally grateful and will share them with other needy teachers!)

Mini-Lesson Focus: Ways to Write in First Grade

Some children have written in kindergarten; some children have not! Depending on their experiences, some children are ready to draw, some children are ready to drite (draw and write), and other children are ready to write some words or sentences. The first writing mini-lessons should show children that there are several different ways they can write in first grade. By doing this lesson, children who don't know how to write words or don't know any letters or the letter sounds can still take part in the Writing Block and "write" their stories.

The teacher talks and writes:

"There are many ways that people tell their stories. Some people use pictures when they write."

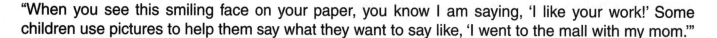

"When you see this smiling face on your paper, you know I am saying, 'I like your work!' Some children use pictures to help them say what they want to say like, 'I went to the mall with my mom.'"

"Another way children write is to use some words they know and draw a picture, too."

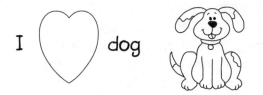

"When children write these words, they usually remember that they wanted to say something like, 'I love my dog. Her name is Panda. She likes to dig in the yard.' "

"Some children know how to write sentences and tell their stories or write about the things they know or the things they do. Here is what one girl wrote: 'I like to go to the mall. I go with my mom. I like to shop at the mall. Sometimes I buy presents.'"

> I like to go to the mall. I go with my
> mom. I like to shop at the mall.
> Sometimes I buy presents.

"So when you write today, there are many ways to do it. You can draw pictures, you can write words, you can drite—draw and write, or you can write using words and sentences. Use what will help you to tell the class and me what you want to tell."

Other Ideas for Showing Children There are Many Ways to Write

Depending upon your first grade class, you may have to do more than one lesson to show the students that there are many ways to write. Here are some variations you can use to let your students know that all different ways of writing are accepted.

Discussing Prehistoric People Who Told Stories with Pictures

Tell your class that long ago, people did not have pencils and paper. People told their stories sitting around a fire at night. These ancient people lived in caves. Sometimes they drew pictures on the walls of their caves. These pictures were later found and now we know how cave men and women lived and what they did long, long ago because their pictures told their stories.

Draw a picture and talk about what people ate a long time ago and how they got their food. Tell the children that people had to pick, catch, or kill their food; they didn't go into stores and buy it. How do we know? They drew pictures which are still there on the walls of some caves!

Discussing Native Americans Who Told Their Stories with Pictures

Tell the children before we lived here, before there was a country called the United States, Native Americans lived here. Many tribes did not have written languages. They did not have paper or anything to write with—no pencils, pens, crayons, or markers, so they told the stories about the wars they had fought. Fathers told their sons and daughters. Children learned about their people (relatives) and their history by listening to stories. Some Native Americans drew pictures of what they did. They drew pictures of how they caught fish (sometimes with arrows, sometimes with nets) and how they killed buffalo to make tents. Their pictures let us know how they lived and what they did. This was another way to tell stories. Draw a simple picture showing a Native American scene and talk about what you are drawing.

Mini-Lesson Focus: Drawing and Writing (Driting)

Early in first grade, the teacher needs to make it "OK" for children to write in whatever way they can. Children need to get in the habit of "telling something" each day and need to become comfortable using pictures, words, and combinations of pictures and words. Teachers model this in their early mini-lessons by drawing something and just writing labels or a few words to go with the pictures. Here is an early-in-the-year driting lesson:

The teacher puts a blank piece of unlined paper on the board or overhead and says:

"Today, I am going to draw and write to show you what I want to tell you about."

The teacher talks about her family as she draws them:

"Here I am. I am wearing my Wake Forest shirt and getting ready to watch the Wake Forest football game."

"Here is my husband. His shirt is Carolina blue and says UNC on it."

"Here is my son, David. David is a North Carolina fan, too and has a matching North Carolina shirt.

"I will write everyone's names under their pictures."

The teacher writes Mrs. Cunningham, Mr. Cunningham, **and** David Cunningham **labels under the appropriate pictures.**

"Sometimes when we write, we use pictures and words to tell the story. Today I wanted to tell you about my family and the teams we cheer for. I used pictures to show the people in my family. I used letters on the shirts to show the teams we cheer for. I used words to write the names of the people in my family."

"Now I want you to draw and write something you want to tell me. You can draw and write about your family, but you can also draw and write about anything else you want to tell. If you do draw and write about your family, your pictures and words will be different from mine because you have a different family."

The teacher gives children unlined paper and encourages whatever level of drawing and writing they can do. After 10 to 15 minutes, she gathers them together in a circle and lets them tell about their "driting."

Other Ideas for Driting

Drawing and Writing about Pets

Children are always interested in pets. Draw and write about pets you have or had when you were a child or of the pets of a relative or friend. As you draw, tell lots of details. Write a label or two to go with your drawings.

"When I was little, I had a cat named Tammy. She was a yellow tiger cat and was quiet and shy."

"She hid when anyone came to visit."

"I am going to write the words Tammy and bed—her favorite hiding place."

Remind children that they should draw and write what they want to tell you. They might write about a pet, but they might also want to write about something entirely different.

Drawing and Writing about a Vehicle

Kids are always interested in things that "go"—bikes, scooters, buses, cars, trucks, etc. Here is a vehicle driting lesson.

" I drive my van to school, but on the weekends, I like to ride my bike. I have a ten-speed green bike with a basket for carrying things home. Riding my bike is fun and good exercise."

Other Kid-Appealing Topics for Driting

Here are some other ideas for drawing and writing about early in first grade:

favorite foods	friends
places (mall, grocery store, YMCA, etc.)	toys
relatives (grandma, cousin, baby sister, etc.)	sports

Driting is an easy entry into writing. Depending on your children, do as many driting mini-lessons as they need to all feel that they can write.

Mini-Lesson Focus: Modeling How to Write a Good Sentence

Writing a good, complete sentence is not an easy skill to learn. First, children need to learn what a good sentence is, and there is really no way to explain what a good sentence is. The best way to help all your children learn how to write good sentences is to do some early mini-lessons in which you only write one sentence, then talk with the children about what makes it a good sentence. A good sentence makes sense to the person who is hearing or reading it!

The teacher draws and thinks aloud:

"Here is my car. I am driving to South Carolina, where I have lots of relatives. I love to go and visit my relatives."

The teacher writes:

I went to South Carolina to visit my cousins.

The teacher asks:

"Who is this sentence about?"

"Where did I go?"

"Who did I visit?"

"Yes, this is a sentence about me. It tells where I went. I went to South Carolina. Who did I go to see? Yes, I went to visit my cousins who live there."

The teacher tells the students that she is going to walk around as they begin drawing their pictures, and she wants each of them to whisper to her the sentence they will write today before they write it. If a child says one complete sentence, she tells him that is a wonderful sentence and moves on to the next child. If a child doesn't tell her a complete sentence, she helps him say a complete sentence before he writes. If any of the children tell her several sentences, she tells them that they have at least two or three good sentences and helps them find the end of each sentence as they say it.

After the children write, the teacher gathers the students together and lets them share their pictures and sentences.

Other Ideas for Modeling How to Write a Good Sentence

Doing More "Draw and Write One Sentence" Mini-Lessons as Needed

Draw a picture of a pet and write a sentence about that pet.

This is *my cat, Tammy.*

Talk about your cat and read your sentence. Ask: What kind of pet do I have? What is my cat's name? Circulate as your children begin to draw and write and have them whisper their sentences to you before they write. Help them to form good, complete sentences. Gather the students together and have them share their pictures and sentences.

Drawing a Picture and Letting Your Children Help You Come Up with a Good Sentence

Draw a picture of you doing something you like to do. Ask your class to help you come up with a good sentence to go with your picture.

Mrs. Hall likes to read books.

Circulate as your children begin to draw and write and have them whisper their sentences to you before they write. Help them to form good, complete sentences. Gather the children together in a circle and have them share their pictures and sentences.

Rereading a Book with One Sentence on a Page and Writing a One-Sentence Response

Show children a book you have recently read to them that has just one sentence on each page. Reread a few pages from the book and help children notice that each page has a picture and one good sentence. For the writing part of your mini-lesson, write one good sentence that summarizes the book. If the book you reread was *Zoo-Looking* by Mem Fox, your summary sentence might be:

Flora looked at many animals, and the animals looked back.

Writing a Sentence and Focusing on Finger Spacing Between Words

If your students are not using spaces between words (they should if you model and talk about it), then focus a mini-lesson on using a finger space between words. Draw a picture of two "stick figure" friends and write:

These are *my friends Pat and Denise.*

Not only will you focus on writing the sentence, but also on the finger space between each of the words. "I begin my sentence with a capital letter and I write the first word **'These'**. I leave a finger space before the next word and then I write **'are'** . . . ."

Mini-Lesson Focus: Expanding One Sentence with Questions

When you can get your children to the point at which most of them are capable of writing at least one good sentence, then they are ready to learn how to add more sentences. Tell the children that once they have one good sentence, thinking of questions will help them think of other sentences.

The teacher thinks aloud and begins to write:

"I am drawing a picture of a birthday cake."

"Now, I will write a sentence to go with my picture. I think I'll write..."

This is a birthday cake.

"This sentence tells about my picture, but I have more to tell. What else should I write? What do you want to know about this birthday cake?"

The teacher leads the children to ask questions, such as:

"Who is the birthday cake for?"

"What kind of cake is it?"

"Who made it?"

"Did you buy it at the store?"

"Who is going to eat the cake?"

The teacher reads the sentence again and then answers the questions as she writes more:

This is a birthday cake. It is for my daughter, Amy. It is for her birthday party. I made it at home last night. It is a chocolate cake. It has pink icing. Pink is Amy's favorite color.

The teacher circulates around the room as the children begin drawing their pictures and writing their first sentences. He asks them questions that will help them think of more sentences. After the children write, the teacher lets the children share their pictures and sentences.

Other Ideas for Expanding One Sentence with Questions

Writing One Sentence that Elicits Questions from Your Students

Write one sentence. Put down your pen (pencil or marker) and say you are done! Write:

> I went to the mall.

The usual response from the children is to ask questions like: Who did you go with? When did you go there? Why did you go there? What stores did you go to at the mall? What did you buy? Answer these questions and add to your story:

> I went to the mall. I went with my friend Pat. We went after school. We went to the big department store. We went to buy school clothes. I bought a new sweater.

Showing a Picture and Writing a Sentence about It

Find a picture in a magazine, tour book, or an old calendar of a place that you know some of your children have visited. Talk about the picture and write a sentence.

> Myrtle Beach is a nice place to visit.

Ask the children some questions about the picture and your sentence: "Who has gone to Myrtle Beach?" "Why did you go there?" "When did you go?" "Who did you go with?" "Where did you stay?" Have different children answer these questions and use the answers to add to your writing. The completed piece might look like this:

> Myrtle Beach is a nice place to visit. Kristen and Matthew went to Myrtle Beach on their vacation. They went in July with their mother and father. They stayed at the Ocean Resort Hotel. They swam in the pool and the ocean. They played in the sand. They had fun!

Showing a Picture and Using the Five "W" Questions

Depending upon your class, you may be able to talk about the five "W" questions (Who? What? Where? When? and Why?). Show a picture of someone and write:

> This is Zannie Murphy.

Show the five "W" questions to your class—they may be on a chart or glove (one on each finger). Answer each question with a complete sentence, and write these sentences after the first sentence.

> This is Zannie Murphy. She is my niece. She likes to play in the sand at the beach. The beach is in Rhode Island. Every summer, Zannie flies to Rhode Island from California. We have a family reunion in Rhode Island every summer.

Using a Book You Have Recently Read to Your Class

Show the class a book you have recently read to them (For example, *The Relatives Came* by Cynthia Rylant) and write one sentence about the book. Ask questions to elicit more sentences from the children.

> <u>The Relatives Came</u> is a story about visiting relatives. The family . . .

Mini-Lesson Focus: Writing Is Telling about Something

Lucy Calkins (1996) says that in Writer's Workshop, "Children write about what is alive and vital and real for them—and other writers in the room listen and extend and guide, laugh and cry and marvel." You, as teachers, have to get that message to your children. Writing is simply telling about things that are important in our lives. Writing is telling things on paper!

The teacher thinks aloud:

"What can I write about today? Let's see. What do I know a lot about? I know about things that have happened to me. What has happened to me lately? Has anything interesting happened to anyone I know? I know! My daughter had a bad dream last night. I used to have bad dreams when I was young, too! I remember when I was four years old, and I had a bad dream. It was so scary that I still remember it to this day! I'll tell you about the time I had a bad dream and then I will write about it."

The teacher tells the class:

"When I was four years old, I had a terrible dream one night. There was an old country store right down the road from my house. I had been to the store many times with my mom. In my dream, my mom and I went to that little, red brick country store. We went to buy sausage. On the way home, we heard noises. They were scary noises. We turned around and a scary thing was following us—we ran. We ran all the way home. It was so scary, I never forgot it. I never wanted to go to the store, alone or with my mom, after that."

Then the teacher writes:

> When I was little, I had a bad dream.
> I went to the store with my mom. A
> scary thing followed us home. I
> never forgot that dream.

The teacher and the children read the writing together:

She reads what she has written with the children and asks: "Can you see a picture of the story in your mind? This is a true story about something that happened in my life. Because I remember it, I can tell you about it and write about it. That's what writing is...telling things. Sometimes, we tell true stories and sometimes we use our imaginations to make up stories."

The teacher reminds the children that the easiest and best way to write a good story is simply to tell a story from their life. "All of us hear stories from our parents, our brothers and sisters, our neighbors, and our friends. When we write, we are telling stories on paper!"

Other Ideas for Writing Is Telling about Something

Reading Stories from the Lives of Other Children

Read a few stories written by children from a previous year, stories that have clearly come from their own lives. (Many teachers make copies of pieces they know they want to use in future lessons.) Ask where the writers got the ideas for their stories. Children usually quickly understand that these are events that really happened in the lives of the writers.

Next, ask your children why they think each writer chose that specific time to write about. The children will usually answer that it was a special time, or a time that was really important to the writer for one reason or another. It might have been a time when the writer had strong emotions or was very excited, scared, happy, or sad.

Finally, ask the children why they think these writers remembered so many details about these times in their lives. Help children to understand that when something makes you have strong emotions or feelings, you don't even have to think about trying to remember it. It's in your mind and heart to stay. That's why telling a story from your life is the easiest way to write—because all of the details and events are already in your mind.

Finding the Stories in Your Life

Make a list of five things from your own life that would make good stories to tell. Read this list with your children and pick one of them to write about today.

Helping Children Find Their Stories

Have children brainstorm things that have happened to them that they will probably never forget. Make a list using some children's names and ideas.

Carly—when I broke my leg

Sam—getting lost

Some children may want to start lists in their writing folders for future reference, "Story Topics from My Life."

Using Ideas from Books Read Aloud

Remind children of a book you have recently read aloud to them, such as *Ira Sleeps Over* by Bernard Waber. Ask them where they think the author got the idea for this book. Write a few sentences about a sleepover you have experienced (or someone you know).

My son Joey, had a sleepover for
his birthday . . .

Mini-Lesson Focus: What To Do about Spelling

What to do about spelling is always a concern among teachers teaching young children to write. Should teachers not worry about correct spelling and let the children feel free to put their ideas on paper? Or, should teachers encourage correct spelling so that the children learn to spell the words correctly? In Four-Blocks classrooms, teachers do both! Four-Blocks teachers tell their young writers not to be concerned about the spelling of words while they are writing their first draft, except for Word Wall words. Many of the high-frequency words placed on the Word Wall—they, was, have, come— are not spelled logically. Spelling these words over and over again the wrong way—thay, wuz, hav, cum—will put these incorrectly-spelled words into the children's automatic memory. From the very beginning of your writing time, encourage the children to stretch out words and put down the letters they hear—except for the Word Wall words. Word Wall words are the only words that you should expect to see spelled correctly. Here is an early mini-lesson on using the Word Wall and stretching out the other words.

The teacher thinks aloud about what to write:

"In a few weeks, we will have our Fall Festival. Today, I am going to write about some of the things we will do at the festival."

The teacher writes and talks about how words are spelled:

Our school will ("**Will** is on the Word Wall." The teacher looks at the Word Wall as she writes **will**.) have ("**Have** is on the Word Wall, too, so I can just look up there to spell **have**.") a fall fes tiv ul. (Stretches out **festival**, pausing between each syllable and writing letters as she says the sounds.) We will (Glances at Word Wall again.) have (Word Wall) good things to eat. We will ("That **will** on the Word Wall is really handy!") play ("Another Word Wall word!") games. You can come (Word Wall) to the fes tiv ul (Stretches **festival** out the same way.) in your cos tooms. (Stretches out **costumes** and writes the sounds she hears.)

The teacher reminds children that in their writing today, they should use the Word Wall to help them spell Word Wall words and stretch out the other words.

Other Ideas for What To Do about Spelling

Teaching Students How to "Read the Room!"

Most first-grade classrooms have the color words, number words, days of the week, and months of the year up on the wall. (If you don't, stop right now and do it!) Every first-grade classroom needs to be a print-rich environment so children can "read the room." First-grade teachers also need to label things in their classrooms, such as the clock, the calendar, the easel, the blackboard, etc. Show the children how to "read the room" and model this in your writing mini-lessons. The children will be able to spell a lot more words (number words, color words, etc.) by looking at the print in your classroom. Don't assume that all children will automatically do this. Many children not only have to be told, but shown how to do this. For some children, you will have to model this over and over throughout the year and remind them of this during writing conferences.

When writing about vehicles, you can model how to use the color words in the room.

My car is green. ("**Green** is on the color chart.") My mom's car is blue. ("Color chart.")
My son's bike is red. ("Color chart.")

When writing about classroom activities, you can model how to use the calendar.

On Monday ("I can spell **Monday** by looking at the calendar.") we go to music.

On Tuesday... ("The calendar helps me spell all the days and months.")

Teaching Students to Use Bulletin Boards and Theme Boards to Spell Words

Most first-grade classrooms have bulletin boards with pictures to go with the unit or theme being studied. Add topic-related words to those boards, and you have another spelling resource readily available to your children.

"Today, I am going to write about our science topic, weather. I bet I will need a lot of words from our weather bulletin board."

The weather ("**Weather** is the title word on the board.") is changing. At night, it is cold.

("**Cold** is the second word on the list of weather words.")

Starting a Chart of Month-Related Words Each Month

Post a chart with the name of the month. Have children brainstorm words related to that month. Write these words and add the children's ideas to the chart as the month continues. Refer to this chart as you write in your mini-lessons.

Using the Rubber Band/Bubble Gum Analogy to Help Students Learn to Stretch Out Words

To help children understand what stretching out words means, you might want to use a rubber band and stretch it as you stretch out some of the words in your mini-lesson. You could also tell students to pretend they are breaking one of Mom's rules by pulling their bubble gum out of their mouths and stretching it out as far as it can go.

In Four-Blocks classrooms, teachers provide lots of in-room print support for spelling and teach children how to use that support and to stretch out words. Except during editing, they **don't** spell words for the children!

Mini-Lesson Focus: Modeling How to Write Using Think-Alouds

Modeling how to write using "think-alouds" is one of the best ways to get first-graders to write. First-graders like to do what the teacher does. If you model something, they will try it! Think-alouds can be used to model any part of writing that you want to teach! We use think alouds to model choosing a topic, referring to the Word Wall, stretching out words, editing, staying on the topic, etc. Anything that helps children write can and should be modeled using think-alouds.

The teacher says:

"Today as I write, I will tell you all about me. Since I am your new teacher, you don't know a lot about me, but you will soon find out!"

The teacher thinks aloud and writes:

"I begin my sentence with a capital letter." (Does each thing as she says it.)

My name is Mrs. Boger.

"I put a capital letter at the beginning of **Mrs.** and **Boger** because names begin with capitals. I end my sentence with a period because telling sentences always end that way."

I have three dawters.

"I begin this sentence with a capital letter. **Have** is on the Word Wall. (Looks at the Word Wall as she writes **have**.) **Three** is on the number word chart." (Looks in that direction as she spells **three**). "**Daughters** is a hard word for first-graders to spell, and when a word is hard to spell, you can stretch it out and write the sounds you hear." (Stretches out and writes **daw** and then pauses, stretches out, and write **ters**.) "I end my sentence with a period."

Their names are Angie, Amie, and Allie.

"I begin this sentence with a capital letter. I know how to spell my daughters' names and remember to use capital letters at the beginnings of their names. I end my sentence with a period."

The teacher continues writing and thinking aloud about capital letters and periods.

I live in a yellow house.

"**Yellow** is over there with the color words."

I drive a green van.

"**Green** is another color word."

I teach first grade at Clemmons Elementary.

The teacher thinks aloud about the process she is using.

She models and talks about using capital letters and periods. Not all children are ready for this, but the ones who are will pick up this information and use it. She also uses this opportunity to str-e-tch out a word or two that the children would not know how to spell and to show them how to use the print in the room to spell words. If she thinks aloud as she writes each day, more and more children will come to understand and use the processes she models and talks about.

Other Ideas for Modeling How to Write Using Think-Alouds

In some mini-lessons, you want to focus on one particular part of the writing process. Here are some think-aloud examples focusing on beginning capital letters and periods, how to spell, and capital letters for names and I.

Using Beginning Capital Letters and Periods

Write something and only think aloud about your use of capital letters and periods. Towards the end of your lesson, stop and ask children what you should put at the end of your sentence and what kind of letter you need to begin the next sentence.

"Today I am going to write about my grandma. I will begin my first sentence with a capital **M**.

My grandma had her birthday last week.

"I end my first sentence with a period and begin my next sentence with a capital **S**.

She is 90 years old.

Toward the end, ask children what you should write: "This is the end of my sentence. What do I need to put here? What kind of letter should I use to start my next sentence?"

Spelling Words

Write something and only think aloud about how you spell words. Stretch out a few of the longer words. Refer to the Word Wall and other print in the room.

"Today I think I will write a story about my trip to the mountains. I just went to the mountains this past weekend, so the details are still in my mind. This is one of those stories in my life that I would like to share with you!"

This weekend, I went ("Went is on the Word Wall.") to the mowntuns. (Stretches out and writes **mown** and then pauses, stretches out, and write **tuns**.) We wanted to see the levz. (Stretches out and writes **levz**.) We saw red, yellow, and orange leaves.

"The color word chart helps me spell all the colors."

Using Capital Letters for Names and I

Write something and only think aloud about how you capitalize names and I. Toward the end of your lesson, stop and ask children what kind of letter you should use to begin names and I.

"This weekend, I went to the fair. I saw lots of you there. Today, I am going to write about who I saw and what they were doing."

When I ("**I** always is a capital letter when it is a word.") was at the fair, I ("Another capital **I**.") saw Brianna and her sister, Lupé. ("I start **Brianna** and **Lupé** with capital letters because they are names.") Brianna and Lupé were looking at the animals.

Continue writing and commenting on capital letters for names and I. Toward the end, ask children what kind of letter to use before writing.

Most of First Grade—Continuing to Write

As the first-grade year continues, the writing time begins to look more like a Writer's Workshop and more like it does at other grade levels. Instead of letting children informally tell about what they were drawing and writing, we begin using an Author's Chair. Most teachers designate one-fifth of the children to share each day. The most struggling writers and the most advanced writers are divided across the days. When the writing time is up, children not sharing gather in front of the Author's Chair and the sharing children line up beside it. One by one, each child reads one piece he has written since his last sharing day. After each child reads, he can call on other students to tell something they liked and to ask questions. The teacher models "nice" comments and good questions and the children soon learn to enjoy their time in the spotlight.

Once Author's Chair is established, most first-grade teachers begin helping children choose pieces to revise, edit, and publish. In most classrooms, children pick one piece to publish when they have three good pieces written. The teacher's time, which has up to this point been spent circulating and encouraging children in their writing, is now allocated primarily to writing conferences in which the teacher helps children revise, edit, and publish.

Once Author's Chair and publishing begin, teachers usually change from half-and-half paper to writing notebooks or writing folders, and drawing is not usually included during the writing time each day. Many teachers let children draw a picture to go with the one piece of writing they plan to share on their day in the Author's Chair, and children do illustrations to go in their published books.

Gradually, children learn how to edit the teacher's and their own writing using an Editor's Checklist. The teacher shows them how to use the checklist in mini-lessons when new items are added, and the children edit the teacher's writing each day using the items on the checklist. Before putting away their writing each day, children do a quick edit of their own writing using the items on the checklist. Their editing is far from perfect. Often, they think their sentences make perfect sense just the way they are. It is hard to end a sentence with appropriate punctuation and begin the next sentence with a capital letter when you are not sure about when one sentence ends and the next one begins. Staying on topic is difficult for many adults and impossible for some first-graders. What is important about the self-edit is not that the students do it perfectly, but that they get in the habit of doing it. As the year goes on, if you are resolute about making just a few mistakes each time you write and having children be your editors and find your mistakes, then all your children will become better—but not perfect—editors of your writing and theirs.

As the year goes on, we continue to teach mini-lessons designed to help children find strategies for deciding what to write about and spelling words. We teach mini-lessons in which we demonstrate how you add on to a piece of writing across several days, rereading and doing a little revision of what was written on previous days. We focus our students' attention on story writing—which for first-graders is almost always a personal narrative—and show them how to have a good beginning, middle, and end. Many children like to write about real things, real people, and things that really happened. We show them how to make a story web and use it to organize an informational piece.

On the following pages are some of the mini-lessons that occupy most of our time in first grade. Just as with the early mini-lessons, we do many lessons for each important strategy. We decide exactly what to focus on by looking at the writing of our children. We often return to the focus of a mini-lesson taught weeks earlier and review that strategy again when the writing of the children shows that although we taught it, many of them didn't learn it! The order of these mini-lessons is one possibility, but teachers who are most successful at teaching writing will tell you that the most important determinant of what you teach (and when) is what your children need. The order and number of lessons you do with this year's class will almost surely not be exactly the same as you will do with next year's class.

Mini-Lesson Focus: Beginning an Editor's Checklist

Once the children are in the habit of writing each day, teachers should begin an Editor's Checklist. Add items to the checklist gradually and show the children how to edit their own pieces using the checklist. What you put first on the checklist depends on your students, your preferences, and your curriculum. Most first-grade teachers begin their checklist with two items: 1. Name and date; 2. Sentences make sense. Here is a first mini-lesson to begin the Editor's Checklist:

The teacher says:

"Soon, we will start publishing some of your writing. Here are some books my first-graders published last year. When we publish, we have to check our writing to make sure everyone can read it and it makes sense. People who check writing are called editors. We are all going to learn to be editors so we can edit our own writing and help each other edit. Editors always have a checklist of things to check for. We are going to begin our checklist with two items." (Writes the two items on a piece of chart paper labeled Editor's Checklist. Discusses each item as she writes it.)

Editor's Checklist

1. Name and Date

2. Sentences make sense

"Each day, after I finish writing, you will help me check to see that I remembered to put my name and date on my writing and to see if all of my sentences make sense. I am going to write for you now, and then you will be my editors. "

The teacher writes, putting her name down but forgetting the date, and including one sentence that doesn't make sense.

Mrs. Hall

Today is Michelle's birthday. She seven years old. Her grandma is baking her a cake. Happy birthday, Michelle!

"Now, I need you to be my editors. Let's check for #1 first. Did I remember to put my name and date?"

The teacher lets the children notice that the date is missing. She adds the date and puts one check at the top to show she has checked for one item.

The teacher has the children read each sentence and gives a "thumbs up" or "thumbs down" to indicate if the sentence makes sense. The second sentence gets a "thumbs down" and the teacher inserts an "is" to make it make sense. When all the sentences are checked, a second check is put at the top of the page. Here is what the edited piece looks like:

Mrs. Hall   ✓ ✓   November 2

Today is Michelle's birthday. She is seven years old. Her grandma is baking her a cake. Happy birthday, Michelle!

Other Ideas for Beginning an Editor's Checklist

Ending Every Mini-Lesson by Having Children Use the Checklist to Edit Your Writing

Once you have begun your editor's checklist, use it every day until all the children become good at checking your writing for the items on the checklist. Use a different color marker to edit your piece so that the editing and check marks stand out. Each day, make one or two errors for your children to correct. Leave your name off, and have one sentence that doesn't make sense on one day. Just leave the date off on the next day. Have one sentence that doesn't make sense on the third day. Continue to make one or two errors each day and have the children find them. They will watch your writing very carefully and delight in finding your mistakes! Some teachers appoint a different child each day as the editor and have this child come up and lead the editing. The child asks the questions (Name and date?) and puts a check at the top of the page. The child then leads the reading of each sentence and the "thumbs up, thumbs down" response. With a little help from the teacher, the child editor fixes the sentence that doesn't make sense and puts a second check at the top of the paper.

Teaching Students to Edit Their Own Writing for the Items on the Checklist

After a week or two of editing your pieces, most children are ready to look at their own writing and check for the things on the checklist. As the writing time is ending, tell children you want them to practice being editors today with their own writing. Many teachers hand out special red "checking" pens or pencils to help the children switch from writing to editing. Have the students read #1 on the checklist and check for their names and dates. If these items are missing, the students add them with their red pens and put checks on the tops of their papers. Next, have them read #2 on the checklist, then read their sentences and give each sentence a "thumbs up" or "thumbs down." Do not expect students to do this perfectly. They often aren't sure where their own sentences end and, they often think all their sentences make perfect sense! It is not reasonable to think that each child will be able to find every sentence that doesn't make sense and fix it. It is reasonable to get students in the habit of rereading their sentences to see if they make sense, and they will find some of the most obvious errors.

Using a Variety of "Not Making Sense" Errors in Your Writing

There are many ways to write a sentence that doesn't make sense.

You can **leave a word out:**

> We went to the museum. We dinosaurs.
> I never knew dinosaurs were so big.

You can **use the wrong word:** (Try to use one that the children confuse and will recognize.)

> We went to the museum. We was dinosaurs.
> I never knew dinosaurs were so big.

You can get distracted and **forget to finish a sentence:**

> We went to the museum. We saw dinosaurs.
> I never knew dinosaurs were so.

Mini-Lesson Focus: Deciding What to Write About (The Topic)

For many children, writing is easy once they decide what they want to write about. In Four-Blocks classrooms, teachers want children to view writing as telling. They stress that when you write, you write about what you want to tell. During Four-Blocks mini-lessons, teachers often "think aloud" about what they might want to "tell today." As the children listen in on the teacher's thinking, they see how he decides what he wants to tell. The children also get some ideas about what they might tell the teacher. Here is what that mini-lesson might look and sound like:

The teacher thinks aloud:

"Let's see. What do I want to tell you about today? I could tell you about the big windstorm we had on Sunday, and how some of the huge trees on our street fell down. I could tell you about the football game I went to Friday night. I know. I was cleaning out a closet this weekend, and I found some of my favorite books from long ago when I was in first grade."

The teacher writes:

Mrs. Cunningham's Favorite Books:

1. Cinderella
2. The Three Little Pigs
3. Are You My Mother?
4. Dr. Seuss's ABC
5. Robert the Rose Horse

As the teacher writes, he and the children talk a little about each book. Many of the children comment that these are some of their favorites, too. Many of the children are not familiar with *Cinderella* and *Robert The Rose Horse*. The teacher tells the children that she will bring in these books tomorrow and read them during Self-Selected Reading.

As the children begin their writing, the teacher notices that some of them are making lists of their favorite books. Part of the purpose of every writing mini-lesson is to help children see that there are many different things people can write about, and many different ways to write. The teacher communicates to the children that writing is primarily to put down on paper something they want to tell. Sometimes, what they want to tell will be on the same topic or in the same form as what the teacher wants to tell. Of course, their writing will always be a little different because it will be their ideas—not the teacher's.

Other Ideas for Deciding What to Write About

Thinking Aloud about a Few Topics You Don't Write About

At least a couple of days each week, begin your writing mini-lesson by thinking aloud about a few topics that you don't write about, but that may spur the thinking of some of your children. If you say that you could write about meeting Jamie in the grocery store and how cute her baby sister is, Jamie may very well be reminded of the meeting and realize that this would be something she would like to tell about. If you say that you could write about how the gerbil got out of his cage and how everyone searched to find him yesterday just before school got out, some of your children who were involved in the hunt will be reminded of that incident, and they might be inspired to write about it. Thinking aloud about a few topics is a subtle way of planting ideas in the minds of your children. Children write best when they are writing about something they know and care about. We don't tell them what they should write about, but we do plant some seeds!

Using Ideas from Sharing

Early in the year in first grade, Four-Blocks teachers don't do a formal Author's Chair, in which one-fifth of the children each day read a piece and get responses to their writing. Rather, the teacher gathers the children and informally asks them, "Who wants to tell us what you were writing about today?" Children hold up their writing and drawing and tell the teacher about it—often telling more than they have actual written words for. This encourages children to see the writing time as telling and allows them all to feel successful as they share their ideas and experiences. Once Author's Chair begins, children continue to get ideas from this daily sharing session. This process in itself gives everyone ideas for writing as they hear what others have written about. You can make this "getting ideas from others" more explicit by doing an occasional mini-lesson in which you add to a class chart of "Things to Write About." Begin your chart one day by remembering some of the great ideas people have shared in the last week. Every few weeks, use your mini-lesson time to add to the chart.

Great Ideas for Writing About:

the pet store	favorite books
soccer games	the substitute teacher
cousins	riding bikes
baby sisters and brothers	video games
big sisters and brothers	swimming

Using Ideas from Books Read

Remind children of a book you read aloud to them or a book the class has read. Write about that book or an idea triggered by that book (for example, *There's a Nightmare in My Closet* by Mercer Mayer).

Mini-Lesson Focus: Procedures for Author's Chair

Early in the year, sharing in first grade is very informal. Gather the children in a circle and let them tell what they were writing and drawing about. As the year goes on, however, you want children to have time to share their pieces and get feedback from the other students. That is when you begin Author's Chair. In the Author's Chair, children share one piece of writing and then ask the other students to make comments (say something nice is the rule!) and ask questions. Most teachers designate one-fifth of the children to share each day. Many teachers use a special chair (rocking chair, big stuffed chair, decorated plastic chair, etc.) for this, but any chair—or even a stool—will do! You can introduce Author's Chair to your students in a mini-lesson. For your mini-lesson, you can write about Writer's Workshop—what you will do each day and why.

The teacher talks about their daily writing time as she writes:

"Today, I am going to write about what we do every day during Writer's Workshop. Every day I write for you and we call this our mini-lesson. During the mini-lesson, I talk and write. I talk about something you need to learn to become better writers. I write something I want to tell you."

> Every day I write for you. We call
> this a mini-lesson.

"After I write, it is your turn to write. You return to your seats, take out your notebooks (or get your writing folders) and begin to write. What do I do while you are writing? Yes, I go around the room and "visit" or "conference" with some of you. We talk about what you are writing about."

> Next, you write and I come around
> and conference with you.

"Usually we end our writing time by making a circle and sharing our writing. Starting today, we will use this chair (Shows the Author's Chair.) to sit in, and everyone will have a special day each week to share. I have made a sign to show who will share on which days. (The sign has Day #1, #2, #3, #4, and #5 and 1/5 of the names are written after each day.) On your day, you sit in our Author's Chair and read one piece that you have written since your last sharing turn."

> We will end our writing time with
> Author's Chair.

"We will start Author's Chair today so if your name is after Day #1 (Reads the names.), look through your notebooks (folders), find a piece you want to read, and get ready to share. Today, I will conference with those who will share today. You can each read your piece to me, and we can talk about it and get ready for Author's Chair."

The teacher is sure to conference today with those who will share in Author's Chair. After the children write and he has spent two to three minutes with each child who will share today, it is time for the first Author's Chair! The teacher models for the children by saying the first "nice" comment ("I liked your story about you playing football. I am glad your team won!") and by asking the first question ("What was the score?").

Other Ideas for Author's Chair

Talking and Writing about What the Children Will Do During Author's Chair

Young children in first grade need to know what to do during Author's Chair. Writing about what they will do during Author's Chair will help some children understand the procedure. Talk and write about this.

In Author's Chair, we read our writing first. Next, we ask for comments. What did we like? Then, we ask questions. What do we want to know more about?

Making a List of "Nice" Comments

Children need to be told that when they share their writing, they will hear "nice" comments first. If you have set this up during your circle and sharing time, this will be an easy progression. Children aren't afraid to share in the Author's Chair if they always hear something positive immediately after reading their writing. Modeling this each day by making the first comment is one way to assure that first grade children pick up this habit. Another way is to make a list of your comments and the children's comment that are appropriate. You can start this chart as your writing mini-lesson, and then add to it every few weeks in future mini-lessons.

Comments from Author's Chair:

"I liked your story about your bike."

"I didn't know you had a dirt bike."

"You must have had fun at the fair."

"You did so many things there."

Making a List of Questions Children Can Ask in Author's Chair

Teach your children to ask appropriate questions during Author's Chair. Modeling this each day by asking the first question is one way to assure that first-grade children learn how to do this. Another way is to make a list of "good questions" and post the list in your classroom. Here is what a list might look like:

Questions We Ask During Author's Chair

"Where did you get the idea for this piece?"

"What is the setting of your story?"

"Can you tell us a summary of your story?" (first, next, last)

"What are you trying to tell us in your piece?"

"Are you planning to add more to your piece?"

"Did you make this up, or did it really happen?"

"How long did it take you to write this?"

"Where did you learn so much about____?"

Mini-Lesson Focus: Adding to Editor's Checklist (Capitals, Ending Punctuation)

In most first grades, it takes about three to five weeks of daily practice for every child to understand how to check their writing for the name and date, and to understand what they are looking for when they read the sentences to see if they make sense. Four-Blocks teachers add something else to the Editor's Checklist when the children have become very quick and automatic at reading the teacher's writing for these two items, and when they are in the habit of checking their own writing (even though they often think some sentences make sense that don't!). What you add to the checklist depends on your students, your preferences, and your curriculum. Here is a mini-lesson (or it might be two) to add items to the Editor's Checklist.

The teacher says:

"You are becoming such good editors that I think it is time to add two more items to our checklist. Here are two other things editors always look for when they are editing a piece of writing." (The teacher adds #3 to the checklist and reminds the children that most of them know to begin sentences with capital letters but sometimes forget.) "All sentences need a mark at the end so we know the sentence is over. We use a period most of the time. But, when we ask a question, we use a question mark. When we say something very exciting, we use an exclamation mark." (The teacher adds # 4 to the list.)

Editor's Checklist
1. Name and date
2. Sentences make sense
3. Beginning capital letters
4. Ending punctuation (. ? !)

"Today, after I finish writing, you will help me check my writing for all four items on the list."

The teacher writes, leaving out one ending punctuation mark and one beginning capital:

Mrs. Cunningham   December 6

My house was very crouded on Thanksgiving. My sister, her huzband, and their three children, Sarah, Jon, and Kevin stayed with us They brought their two big dogs, Bixby and Atticus. we had a good time but there were people and dogs everywhere!

"Now, I need you to be my editors. Let's check for #1 first. Did I remember to put my name and date? Good, we can put one check at the top. Now, when we check the sentences we are going to check for #s 2, 3, and 4. Let's read my first sentence together. Show me a "thumbs up" if it makes sense. Now, show me a "thumbs up" if I remembered the punctuation. Good. Now before we read the next sentence, we need to see if it has a capital."

The children continue to read each sentence and give a "thumbs up" or "thumbs down" to indicate if the sentence makes sense and if it has ending punctuation. They then look to see if the next word begins with a capital letter and read that sentence. The second sentence gets a "thumbs up" for making sense, but a "thumbs down" for ending punctuation. The period is inserted. The first letter of the last sentence is changed to a capital **W**. The edited piece has four checks at the top of the page.

Other Ideas for Adding to Editor's Checklist (Capitals, Ending Punctuation)

Ending Every Mini-Lesson by Having Children Use the Checklist to Edit Your Writing

Continue to use your editor's checklist **every day**. Do not make more than one or two mistakes, but include all the different possibilities on different days. Leave your name off and have one sentence that lacks ending punctuation one day. Have one sentence that doesn't begin with a capital letter on the next day. Have one sentence that doesn't make sense on the third day. Cluttering up your writing with a lot of errors is confusing to many children who can't keep up with them all. If you only make one or two errors, they will pay close attention to your writing and notice your mistakes! Keep the editing moving at a quick pace. Checking for the name and date should be very quick and automatic by now. Have the children read each sentence only once. At the end of each sentence, check to see that it makes sense and has ending punctuation. Look at the letter that begins the next sentence before reading it. If you only make one or two errors each day, adding these two items to the checklist will not add much time to the daily editing process.

Teaching the Children to Edit Their Writing for the Items on the Checklist

After a week or two of editing your pieces for the four items, tell the children that you want them to edit their own writing for all four items. They should continue to check for the name and date, and then read their pieces one time, stopping at each sentence and asking themselves if it makes sense and has ending punctuation and then looking at the first letter of the next sentence before reading it. Again, do not expect the students to do this perfectly. If they are not sure about where their sentences end, they won't notice that they have no ending punctuation or that the next word does not begin with a capital. What you want is for them to get in the habit of rereading their pieces for these items. As the year goes on and they help you edit your piece every day, their "sentence sense" will develop, and they will become better and better at editing their own pieces.

Not Confusing the Children by Putting the Wrong Ending Punctuation

It is much too early for most first-graders to notice that you have put a question mark when you really needed a period or that a surprising sentence should have an exclamation mark instead of a period. Usually, it only confuses first-graders if you put the wrong punctuation mark. When you are leaving off ending punctuation, you should, however leave off all three marks (but not in the same lesson!) When the children notice that you forgot the ending punctuation at the end of a sentence, such as:

Who will help me clean my room

ask them what kind of mark you should use and then put the appropriate mark there (question mark). You might leave off an exclamation mark in a sentence such as:

Suddenly the lights went out

They should notice that you have forgotten your ending punctuation and together you decide that an exclamation mark is needed.

When you use all three types of ending punctuation in your daily writing, leave off all three types on different days, and let children help you decide which one to use, most children will become good at using the appropriate ending punctuation.

Mini-Lesson Focus: Adding on to a Piece of Writing

Children need to learn how to add on to a piece of writing. Just as for everything we teach them about writing, the most effective way to teach adding on is to model it. Begin by writing a story one day—thinking aloud, talking, and writing. The next day, you can model how to revisit what you wrote, read it over, and add on to it. Taking two or three days to write about the same topic gives your children permission to do this. Your most avid writers always have more to say than they can write in one day. Your struggling writers need more than a day if they are ever going to finish a piece! Encouraging children to take as many days as they need to write a piece is one way to make your Writing Block multilevel.

The first day, the teacher thinks aloud about the field trip and writes:

Our Field Trip

Yesterday, our class went to Old Salem. We rode the bus there. Mrs. Stewart, T. J.'s mother, went with us. We vizited many places. We went to the bakery, the church, and the muzeum.

The next day, the teacher adds on:

The teacher revisits by thinking aloud, talking about, and rereading what he wrote. He takes out the transparency of (or turns his chart tablet to) the previous day's writing. "Now, let's see where I started this yesterday. It was all about our field trip to Old Salem. I wrote about how we got there, who went with us, and the buildings we visited. Let's read it together." The teacher reads his writing with the children.

Then, he says, "Did I tell everything we did? No, I have lots more to tell. I could tell what we saw at the bakery, what we saw in the church, and what we saw at the museum. I could tell about the candle-light tea we went to. Today, I am going to add on to my piece about our field trip." Then, the teacher thinks aloud once again and adds:

In the bakery, we saw people making cookies and bread. The church was decorated with canduls and wrethes. In the museum, we saw clothes people wore and tools they used long ago.

To finish this, the teacher wants and need a third day:

The teacher still has not written about the candlelight tea, although he talked about it the second day. He wants to reread his writing from the first two days and finish his piece on a third day.

After writing each day, the teacher dismisses by task:

The teacher encourages and reminds children about adding on by dismissing them from the mini-lesson group by task, "Those who are still writing on a piece can return to their seats. Those who plan to start a new piece of writing can go back to their seats."

Other Ideas for Adding on to a Piece of Writing

Writing about Something that Happened to You and Stopping Before the Ending

Think aloud and begin to write your story:

> Yesterday was a terrible, horrible day. First, I overslept. I was supposed to have my dawter at school early. I was supposed to meet with the principul. I woke my children up late. They were grumpie because I was rushing them.

The next day reread your writing, then ask, " When I stopped yesterday, I had only just started writing about my morning. Do you think I am finished with my story?" Continue to write:

> I got to school late . . .

Writing a Class Summary about a Story You Have Read in Guided Reading

Begin a summary of a story your class read during Guided Reading (for example, *There's an Alligator under My Bed* by Mercer Mayer). Write the beginning one day:

> This story begins with a boy telling us there used to be an alligator under his bed. But, nobody else saw it. He...

Add the middle the next day.

> The boy puts food out to catch the alligator. He puts . . .

The end can be written on the third day.

> The alligator followed the food to the garage. Now, Dad has a problem.

Sharing Students' Writing and Helping Them Add On

Make a transparency of a child's story that could be added on to. Read the story together as a class. Then, as a class, add on to the story and finish it together!

Finishing a Story Started in the Teacher Read-Aloud

After reading the beginning of a book that was too long to finish in one teacher read-aloud session, write a summary of the story so far. The next day, write the ending of the story. Ask the students what they think will happen. Think aloud and write their ending. Compare their writing, and how you ended the story to the author's ending after you finish reading the book to the class. Sometimes, teachers and first-graders think of endings that are just as good or better than the author's. And sometimes it is hard to better the original!

Mini-Lesson Focus: Spelling (The Word Wall Can Help You Spell Other Words)

In most classrooms, children are learning so much about writing that they have to be reminded of some things that they learned earlier in the year. They are also ready to learn how to do more. Spelling is one of those areas where many children need constant reminders of the different ways they can get help to spell words from our room—both from the Word Wall and the print teachers have up in classrooms. The print in the room has expanded and some has changed; especially the theme boards. Although you have stretched a word or two out in most of your mini-lessons, some children may still need encouragement to do this. The middle of the year is a time to review the sources of correct spelling in the room and add a new one—using Word Wall words to spell other words that have the same spelling patterns.

The teacher thinks aloud about what to write:

"We have been learning all about winter, and the changes that occur in winter. I am going to write about winter today!"

The teacher talks, focusing on how to spell words, and writes as she talks:

Winter

("This is the name or title of what I am writing today. I know how to spell it because it is right there on our theme board.")

In winter ("Another theme board word.") it gets colder. ("**Cold** is on the theme board, too. It is the word **cold** with the ending **er**.") We (Glances at Word Wall.) wear jackets (Stretches out **jack-ets** and gets it right.) and wul (Stretches out **wool** and gets it wrong!) coats ("Another theme board word.") to keep warm. Birds fly ("Sounds like it ends with **i**, but I know it is like the word **my** on the Word Wall and ends with a **y**.") south in winter. Animals ("Another theme board word.") hunt for food. We play (Word Wall) inside. ("I know how to spell **in** and **side** rhymes with **ride**—a Word Wall Word—so I just change the beginning sound").

The teacher does a "quick edit" and reviews all the ways she used the Word Wall to help her spell.

The teacher ends this lesson with a "quick" edit, circling the "one" misspelled word, and reviewing the different ways she used the print in the room to get so many words spelled correctly in her writing today. She is sure to emphasize that the children have one more way to help them now—using Word Wall words to spell words that rhyme with them and have the same spelling patterns.

Other Ideas for Spelling

Looking at Their First Drafts and Reteaching Them How to "Read the Room"

Are your children using the color words, number words, and days of the week? If their writing shows that they are forgetting to use the print in the room, do a mini-lesson emphasizing this. If things have changed, and it is time for a new schedule to be written, write it for your mini-lesson. "Today, I will write our new schedule. I know you can help me spell many of the words correctly by telling me where in our room I can find them."

Our Schedule ("Let me copy that word from the old schedule!")

Monday - Music at 10:30 ("I can copy that from the old schedule, or I can look at the calendar to get the word **Monday** spelled correctly. I can find the word **Music** on the old schedule—not under Monday, but it is there. **Music** begins like **Monday**.")

Tuesday - Art at 1:00 ("Where can I find the word **Tuesday**?")

Looking at Their First Drafts and Teaching Them How to Write Children's Names Correctly

Are the children in your class writing the names of their classmates correctly? If not, teach them to use the names on the Word Wall. Many first-grade teachers begin their Word Walls with the children's names. Other teachers have special names boards, with the names of the children and other important school people—often with accompanying photos. However you do it, you need to display all the children's names somewhere in the room and teach the students to look there for the spelling of the names—or when they want to write a word that begins with the same sound as they hear in someone's name. Refer to these names when doing your mini-lesson.

Yesterday we acted out the story, The Door Bell Rang. Molly ("I can spell the name **Molly** by looking at the names on my Word Wall. **Molly** is the second name under the **M**.") *was the mother. Ryan* ("I can spell the name **Ryan** by looking at the names on my Word Wall, also. His name is under the **R**.") *and Suzanne* ("I can spell her name by looking at the names on my Word Wall. What letter is the name **Suzanne** under?") *were her children. Grandma was . . .*

Looking at Their First Drafts and Teaching Them How to Stretch Out Words They Don't Know

Some children are afraid to misspell words. (Maybe they have gotten this message from their parents or a teacher!) Tell them that when you were in first grade—just their age—you couldn't spell all the words you wanted to write. Most six-year-olds can't! So, what do you do at age six? When a word isn't in the room or on the Word Wall (and all words are not up there; especially the words we use just once in awhile) then you have to do stretch it out and write what you hear. You can always use your "ear "or "sound" spelling! S-t-r-e-t-ch-ing out words does not mean you repeat the sounds over and over. Stretching out words means you say them s-l-ow-ly and write the sounds you hear. When children write repeated letters, like **zzzzoo**, they are usually isolating the sounds—not stretching them out. In your mini-lessons, you can model how to stretch out words without isolating the sounds.

The Zoo (Stretches out and writes **zoo**.)

We read Zoo-Looking. We read about tigers . . . (Stretches out **ti-ger-s**.)

Mini-Lesson Focus: Adding to Editor's Checklist (Circle Misspelled Words)

In most first grades, teachers add something else to the Editor's Checklist when the children have become very quick and automatic at reading the teacher's writing each day for the items already on the checklist. When they are in the habit of checking their own writing to see if sentences make sense (even though they often think some sentences make sense that don't!) and are checking for beginning capital letters and ending punctuation, you are ready to add something new to the list. If you have been working hard on spelling, then it is time for the children to begin to check their writing and circle any words they think are misspelled. Here is a mini-lesson to add this item to the Editor's Checklist.

The teacher says:

"You are becoming such good editors that I think it is time to add another item to our checklist. We have been working on spelling, and editors always check spelling when they are editing a piece of writing."

The teacher talks aloud and writes:

The teacher adds #5 to the checklist and reminds the children that most of them know which words they didn't know how to spell, couldn't find in the room, and had to stretch out when they were writing. When we are editing, we circle these words. If we want to publish this piece, we will need to get help to spell these words correctly.

Editor's Checklist

1. Name and date
2. Sentences make sense
3. Beginning capital letters
4. Ending punctuation (. ? !)
5. Circle misspelled words

"Today, after I finish writing, you will help me check my writing for all five items on the list."

The teacher writes, leaving out one ending punctuation mark and one beginning capital letter and stretches out and misspells two words.

Mrs. Boger   December 6

We will go to the awditorrium today. The fourth grade children will sing. Mrs. Holiday will play the peano the second grade children will do a play about how we celebrate the holidays. We will listen quietly.

The children and the teacher read the piece together, add the missing period and capital letter, and circle **awditorrium** and **peano**.

Other Ideas for Adding to Editor's Checklist (Misspelled Words)

Ending Every Mini-Lesson by Having the Children Use the Checklist to Edit Your Writing

Continue to use your Editor's Checklist **every day**. Do not make more than one or two mistakes in a category, but include all the different possibilities. Write each day and do a "quick edit" each day.

Having the Children Bring Red Pencils and Pieces of Writing to the Mini-Lesson

Children love to be the editor. They especially love to edit their own writing. Tell them they are going to be teachers today. Let them use a red pen or pencil and pretend they are the teacher, and they are editing. Go through each item on the checklist and have them check their papers. Doing a few whole-class lessons helps the children become better at self-editing. Young children will look more closely for mistakes if they have a special pen or pencil to use and if you make a big deal out of how good they are at editing. When you conference individually with students, you can remind them of how they did this with you and the class.

After Doing a Mini-Lesson, Choosing a Child to be Your Editor

When students get good at checking their own writing, let one of them become your editor. Some teachers buy a visor and let the student editor wear the "editor's hat" when they are chosen to be the student editor. Children like to find the mistakes the teacher has made when writing. They like to know they can do this—and the other children like to watch closely to make sure they do!

Reinforcing your Spelling Mini-Lessons During Conferences

What you say when you conference will make an impression on your students. When you brag on their spelling ("I liked the way you got all your Word Wall words right!" "I wondered how you got yesterday spelled right. You did just what we talked about in our mini-lesson—you read the room!") It is amazing how well children will use the strategies you teach in your mini-lessons if you reinforce them during your writing conferences.

Mini-Lesson Focus: Choosing a Title for Your Writing

In Four-Blocks classrooms, teachers want children to view writing as telling. Four-Blocks teachers stress that when you write, you write about what you want to tell. As the children begin to write, they often put names or titles on their writing. The teacher writes about the class's field trip and titles it, "Our Field Trip." The child wants to tell about her bike and she writes, "My Bike," at the top of her paper. It's time to talk about titles and how we choose them—and when.

The teacher thinks aloud:

"Let's see. What do I want to tell you about today? I could tell you about the new book I just bought. I think I will save that to read to you later today. I could tell you about the basketball game I went to at the coliseum on Saturday. My team lost, so I don't think that would be fun to write about. I know, I will tell you about the sweet potato tarts I baked last night. I baked 40 of them!"

The teacher thinks aloud and writes:

"Since this is going to be about my sweet potato tarts, I will write that first as my title." She then writes,

Sweet Potato Tarts

at the top of her transparency (or chart paper) to begin her writing. Next, she thinks aloud about what she did, why she did it, and how to write it. "Every year at this time, I make sweet potato tarts for my friends. They taste a lot like pumpkin tarts, but my friends say they like them better. Sweet potatoes grow in the ground like other potatoes. This is the time of year when you find them in the stores or at the farmers' market. This year, a friend gave me a big bag of them that he got from his garden. I think it was a hint to make the sweet potato tarts! I will start my writing today by telling that." She then talks and writes:

> Yesterday, a friend gave me a big bag of sweet potatoes. I usually bake sweet potato tarts for my friends. I cooked the sweet potatoes and added the other ingredence. ("I stretch that word out.") Then I poured the filling into the little pie shells and baked them in the oven. When they were done, I devided ("I stretch that word out.") them into groups of 8. I gave 8 tarts to each of my friends and saved 8 for my family.

The teacher and the class read the story and talk about the title:

"I wrote the name, or the title, first. Sometimes you know what you will write about and put that on your paper at the beginning. At other times, you have an idea but are not sure what a good title will be. You can wait until after you have finished writing and see exactly what you have written, and then, come up with a title. After you finish your writing, it is always a good idea to reread your writing and say to yourself, 'Is this a good title for my writing?' Let's do that now."

"'**Sweet Potato Tarts**' is one name for this piece. What else could I have named this?" The children give her titles: "**Baking Sweet Potato Tarts**," "**Sweet Potato Tarts for My Friends**," etc. The teacher can let the class vote on the best title or she can decide which title she thinks is best. If she decides another name is better, she can change the title.

Other Ideas for Choosing a Title

Writing and Having the Children Think of the Title

Write about something you have done and have the children come up with three to four possible titles. Choose or vote on which is the best. Put that title at the top of your paper. You could write about going to a basketball game to see Wake Forest University play against the University of North Carolina and Wake Forest winning. The children may give you these possible titles: "Wake Forest Wins;" "Wake Forest and North Carolina Play Basketball;" "Wake Forest Beats North Carolina;" "A Great Game." Since all the titles are good, let the children vote to decide. They choose "Wake Forest Wins." You write that at the top of the piece.

Choosing a Title and Writing, Then Deciding the Title Needs to Be Changed

Choose a title like, "My Dog." Write about your pet dog (or someone in the room's dog or cat).

> My dog Aussie likes to dig. He digs in
> the backyard. He digs up the grass.
> He digs big holes. We think he might
> dig a hole to China some day!

Decide that this story is not all about your dog, but about something your dog likes to do—he likes to dig. With your class, brainstorm some different titles: "My Digging Dog," "Aussie Likes to Dig," "My Dog Digs Holes." Choose the one you and the class like best. If it is "My Digging Dog," then draw a line through the old title and write the new one above it.

Choosing a Title for an Informational Piece You Write

As teachers we often work with "stories" to choose a title for, but we need to do this for informational pieces, also. Write about winter and have the children title the piece.

Choosing a Title and Writing an Informational Piece, Then Deciding the Title Needs to Be Changed

Choose a title ("Winter") and write all about animals hibernating in winter. Decide that this is all about animals hibernating, not just winter. Brainstorm with your class a list of new titles for this piece. Choose the one you and your class like best. Draw a line through the old title and write the new title above it.

Writing about a Book You Have Read to the Class and Choosing a Title

Write about a book you have read during a recent teacher read-aloud. Focus on the character. If you read *Alexander and the Terrible, Horrible, No Good, Very Bad Day* by Judith Viorst, you could write about all the bad things that happened to Alexander. Decide on a title for this story. It may be something like: "Why Alexander's Bad Day Was So Bad."

Mini-Lesson Focus: Procedures for Publishing

By now your first-grade students are in the habit of writing each day, have learned to "add on" to a piece, have learned to spend several days writing a piece, and have learned about editing. Now, you are ready for the part of Writer's Workshop that first-grade children absolutely love—publishing! Publishing—which really means making writing "public"—gives children a reason to revise and edit. In first grade, many children want to publish everything. Most teachers find it easier and more manageable if the children don't publish every piece they write. In most classrooms, children are allowed to choose one piece to publish when they have three completed pieces. Once publishing begins, the teacher changes how she uses her time while the children write. Instead of "circulating and encouraging," teachers spend longer periods of time "conferencing and editing" with children who are ready to publish. How do you do it? Once again, you model it!

Day One of Publishing

The teacher shows the class three pieces she has written, thinks aloud, and says:

"I have written many pieces this year. I have written about the things I like to do, the places I have gone with my family, and the things we are studying about. Today, I am going to look at three of the pieces I have written and decide which one I want to publish. When we publish in this class, we make a book. We put the book in the book basket so everyone can read it. At the end of the year, you get to take the books you have published home. Let's look at the three pieces I think are my best." The teacher then puts three pieces on the overhead projector (or show three pieces from the chart tablet).

The teacher reads and discusses each of the three pieces:

One by one the teacher displays and reads each of the three pieces and discusses what she likes about each piece. "I like this one called *My Digging Dog.* I think it would make a good book, and I know just how I will illustrate the pages. I think many of you would enjoy this book because you enjoyed that story when I wrote it." "I really liked *Sweet Potato Tarts,* but I am not so sure everyone liked it as much as I did. I want to publish something that most of the class would like to read." I like *Animals Hibernate in Winter,* too. It is very hard to choose, but I think for my first book, I will choose *My Digging Dog.*

The teacher returns to the chosen piece and revises and edits it:

"The first thing I want to do is to think if there is anything I want to change about my story. I like it, so I don't want to change much, but read it with me one time and see if you can think of anything that would make it a little better." The children and teacher read *My Digging Dog* together and decide to change the word **big** to **huge**. The teacher crosses our **big** and writes **huge** above it. The piece has already been edited, but there are more items on the checklist now than there were at that time. The children and teacher do a quick reedit. The teacher circles two words that she had stretched out to spell. She then writes the correct spelling above these. "We don't worry about the spelling of words not in the room on the first draft," she reminds them. "But, I will help you fix the spelling of every word when you are making a book, so that everyone can read it easily."

Procedures for Publishing (Days Two through Five)

Day Two of Publishing

The first publishing lessons take more than one day to model. The first day you choose, revise, and edit your piece. The next day, you model what you do next—divide the selection into the number of pages you have to write on and begin to copy your piece over in your "very best handwriting." (Often teachers print the first book for students, especially if they think the author's handwriting might make it hard for other children to read. Some teachers edit with the child and then type the text.) You need to do this lesson on the actual book. Bring the children up close to you so that they can see what you are doing. Let them read from the overhead or chart each sentence and watch you write it in your book.

The teacher thinks aloud, talks, and writes the title page:

"I start with my title page and write the title here in my very best handwriting, **My Digging Dog**. Underneath the title I write the word **by** and then write my name, **Mrs. Hall**, because I am the author of this book. You will write your name because you will be the author of your book. Write one sentence—in your best handwriting—on each page."

(Children with 10 sentences might have made a 10-page book. If someone has 14 sentences, the teacher helps them decide how to put two sentences on some pages. It is a good idea not to go over 10 pages for first-grade books.)

My dog Aussie likes to dig.
He digs in the backyard.
He digs up the grass.
He digs huge holes.
We think he might dig a hole to China some day!

Day Three of Publishing—The Teacher Illustrates the Book

The teacher turns to each page, thinks aloud about what she might draw, then draws a picture that goes with the text on the page.

My dog Aussie likes to dig. "On this page, I should draw my dog Aussie, and I should draw him digging! On the next page . . ."

Day Four of Publishing—The Teacher Makes the Cover, Puts the Book Together, and Reads It

The teacher writes the title and author on the cover and illustrates the cover. She talks about the complete book and how carefully she copied over every page. (Some children will write the final draft just like they wrote the first draft, so this part needs to be stressed; copy the edited copy!) The teacher keeps some correction fluid on hand for children if they write final copies in pen. If the students write on the computer, she remembers to "check it" before they press "Print."

Day Five of Publishing—The Teacher Writes the "All about the Author" Page

The teacher tells about herself and writes a page about the author—her.

Mrs. Hall teaches first grade. She has two daughters. She likes to read. She likes to write books, too!

She lets the children know that she will interview them and write this page when they publish their books.

Mini-Lesson Focus: Adding to Editor's Checklist (Capitals–Names and Places)

You have been writing, editing, and have started to publish with your first-grade students. If most of your children can check for the items on the Editor's Checklist, it is time to add something new to the checklist. Many first-grade teachers now focus their children's attention on capital letters for names of people and places. Because of your modeling, many of your students may be using these capitals. Here is a mini-lesson to add this item to the Editor's Checklist.

The teacher thinks aloud and adds another item to the checklist:

"You are becoming such good editors that I think it is time to add another item to our checklist. Here is another thing editors always look for when they are editing a piece of writing." The teacher adds number six to the checklist and says, "Most of you know this and do this when writing. We use capital letters at the beginnings of people's names and the names of places. You all write your names beginning with capital letters. My name is Mrs. Boger, and I always begin that with a capital letter. The name of our school is Clemmons Elementary, and we always begin that with a capital letter. The name of our mall is Hanes Mall; we begin that with a capital letter, too. When we write the name of people or places, we use a capital at the beginning." (The teacher adds #6 to the list.)

Editor's Checklist

1. Name and date
2. Sentences make sense
3. Beginning capital letters
4. Ending punctuation (. ? !)
5. Circle misspelled words
6. Capital letters for names and places

"Today, after I finish writing, you will help me check my writing for all six items."

The teacher talks and writes:

The teacher writes, leaving out one period and failing to capitalize **Amy** and **Charlotte**.

Mrs. Boger   January 26

Last weekend, amy and I went to charlotte. We went to see the Hornets play basketball There was a large crowd there. The game was very exciting. The Hornets won!

The teacher and class do a "quick edit:"

The teacher and the class read each sentence for sense and ending punctuation, and then look to see if there are any names of people or places. The teacher helps the children notice that names of professional basketball teams, like the Hornets, also need capital letters.

Other Ideas for Adding to Editor's Checklist (Capitals—Names and Places)

Ending Every Mini-Lesson by Having Children Use the Checklist to Edit Your Writing

Continue to use your Editor's Checklist **every day**. Only make a few mistakes, but include all the different possibilities in your different lessons. You might write about places where it snows a lot, and the cities or states you mention would need capitals at the beginning.

> The weather channel had pictures of a bad snowstorm around the great lakes. They showed pictures of chicago, Detroit, and . . .

Writing about a City and Place in the Mountains or Desert and Having the Students Edit It

> It snowed in the mountains (Some children might think this needs a capital—you need to explain that if it was the name of the mountains, like Appalachian Mountains, it would need a capital, but not with just the word mountain.) last night. We will go to blowing rock this weekend. There is a great place to ski there. It is called Mt. Snow. Have you ever been skiing there?

Writing a Weather Article about Your Area and Having a Student Be Your Editor

The teacher thinks aloud and writes:

> A cold front is coming from the west. It crossed the Rocky Mountains and moved across the plains ("This is not the name of the Plains area of the United States and doesn't need a capital.") Snow is coming to the St. Louis area and all the way to the mississippi river . . . ("Names need capitals.")

Writing with Lots of People's Names and Having a Student Edit It

Write a story about the children in your class, or neighborhood, or the teachers at school. Leave one or two names without capitals. Do a quick edit, noting the capital letters you used and the ones you forgot.

> Mrs. joyner sent me a picture of her three children. She has a son named Jake, a daughter named Tess, and a new baby boy named samuel Herbert Joyner.

Talk about how **son, daughter**, and **baby** don't need capitals, but **Mrs. Joyner, Jake, Tess**, and **Samuel** do need capital letters because they are people's names.

Write about a Book and Talk about the Authors and Characters

When writing about a favorite book, you will use lots of capitals.

> One of my favorite books is <u>Stellaluna</u> by janelle cannon. It is. . .

Mini-Lesson Focus: Writing a Story (Beginning, Middle, End)

Teachers need to remind their students that when they read books aloud, they are often "stories" with a beginning, middle, and end. Students also need to be reminded that during Guided Reading, one thing they talk about is the beginning, middle, and end of the story—no matter how long it takes the class to read the story. Now, during Writing, the teacher will again talk about writing "stories" that have a beginning, middle, and end.

The teacher thinks aloud about what to write:

"I could write a story about visiting my sister, who lives in the desert. My airplane trip would begin that story. I could write about a basketball game I watched. I know how that story would end—with my favorite team winning. I could write about one of my favorite books, *Stellaluna*. Since we are talking about the beginning, middle, and end of stories, I will write about *Stellaluna*."

The teacher thinks aloud and writes:

The teacher talks about the capital letters, ending marks, spelling, and what happened at the beginning, middle, and end as she writes:

Stellaluna

This story begins with Stellaluna falling from her mother's wings. She lands in a bird's nest. In the middle Stellaluna is raized (Stretches that word out.) by the birds. She hangs upside down. The birds do not. Stellaluna has truble (Stretches that word out.) learning to fly like the birds do. The story ends with Stellaluna finding her mother and learning that she is not a weird bird. She is a bat!

The teacher does a quick check with the Editor's Checklist and then discusses what happened at the beginning, middle, and end.

She adds a period to the third sentence, and circles **raized**. Next, she discusses what she wrote about the beginning at the beginning, what she wrote about the middle in the middle, and how she ended her story by writing about the end. (The teacher might want to take out a story map or call the children's attention to it. "You can use a story map to help you write!")

```
┌─────────────────────────────────────────────┐
│                 Story Map                    │
│                                              │
│   Characters   _____  │
│                                              │
│   Setting      _____  │
│                                              │
│   Beginning    _____  │
│                                              │
│   Middle       _____  │
│                                              │
│   End          _____  │
│                                              │
└─────────────────────────────────────────────┘
```

Other Ideas for Writing a Story (Beginning, Middle, End)

Writing about Something That Happened to You (It Must Have a Beginning, Middle, and End)

One thing that teachers write about all the time is events that happen to them or their children. Choose that familiar topic, think aloud, and write your story with a clear beginning, middle, and end. You will probably need to add on to your piece across several days.

Fishing with Grandpa

I used to love to go fishing with my Grandpa.
One time we went to the Yadkin River. At first
we just sat there trying to get a fish. Then, I
felt a . . .

Writing about One of Your Students (It Must Have a Beginning, Middle, and End)

Have a private conversation with the student before you write about him or her and what happened at the beginning, middle, and an end. This story allows you to review capitals for names and places.

Ashley's Trip to Disney World

Ashley went to Disney World with her mother,
father, and brother, carl. They flew to Orlando,
Florida. Her father rented a car. They stayed
at a hotel outside of Disney World. The first
day, they went to Magic Kingdom. They rode
all the rides. The next day they went to
Epcot Center . . .

Letting the Class Help You Construct a Story Based on a Story They All Know and Enjoy

Review a favorite story such as *The Three Pigs* or *The Doorbell Rang*. Let the class help you decide on new characters (perhaps some of them!) and some new events. Write important details—including the beginning, middle, and an end—on a story map. Let the class help you write the story across several days of mini-lessons.

Once upon a time, there were three little
puppies that lived with their grandma in a tiny
little house . . .

Mini-Lesson Focus: Modeling Ending Punctuation Marks Using Think-Alouds

Modeling how to write using "Think-Alouds" is one of the best ways to get first-graders to understand the writing process. You should do this almost every day during your mini-lesson. When focusing on the different punctuation marks that end different types of sentences, think-alouds are a good way to do it. Teachers discuss the different types of ending marks when they do shared reading with big books. When modeling writing, the teacher has been putting periods at the end of sentences that tell; question marks at the end of questions; and exclamation marks at the end of sentences that show excitement. In this lesson, we will focus on those ending marks as we write in our mini-lesson today.

The teacher thinks aloud and writes:

"Today as I write, I am going to talk about the different marks I put at the end of my sentences. Sometimes, I tell something like, 'I have three daughters' and then I will write it."

I have three dawters.

"I begin my sentence with a capital letter. I use the Word Wall to spell **have**. I use the number words on the chart to write **three**. I stretch out and write **dawters** because it is not a Word Wall word, and most six-year-olds cannot spell it. I put a period at the end of that sentence because periods go at the end of sentences that tell you something."

"Sometimes I ask questions when I write, 'Do you know what we did yesterday?' "

The teacher writes:

Do you know what we did yesterday?

"When I write a sentence like that, I begin with a capital letter and use the Word Wall and the room to help me spell words (model this), but when I get to the end, I put a question mark because I have asked a question."

"Sometimes I write a sentence about something exciting, like 'We went to a party!' "

The teacher writes:

We went to a party!

"When I am writing about something exciting, I still begin the sentence with a capital. I still use the Word Wall, words in the room, and stretch out words for spelling, but I end with an exclamation mark."

The teacher adds sentences and thinks aloud about the different ways to end each of these sentences.

"I am going to add some sentences onto my writing." (The teacher writes each sentence, discusses what mark is needed at the end, and then puts it there.)

We went to Mrs. Marion's house. ("This sentence **tells** where we went, so I put a period at the end of it.") All my friends were there! ("This sentence lets you know I was **surprised** that all my friends were there, so I put an exclamation mark at the end of this one.") Did you know yesterday was my birthday? ("This sentence **asks** a question, so I put a question mark at the end of it.")

Writing Mini-Lessons for First Grade: The Four-Blocks® Model

Other Ideas for Modeling Ending Punctuation Marks Using Think-Alouds

Putting a Period at the End of a Sentence

In some mini-lessons, you want to focus on one particular type of sentence. The first type of sentence that children learn about is the sentence that tells something. It ends with a period ("stop sign"). Here are some think-aloud examples focusing on sentences that tell something.

People celebrate the holidays in different ways. ("This needs a period.")

Some people put up a Christmas tree. ("This needs a period.")

Other people light candles. ("This needs a period.")

Many people have special food and special meals. ("This needs a period.")

Families gather together to celebrate the holidays. ("This needs a period.")

Putting a Question Mark at the End of a Question

"Sometimes we ask questions in our writing. When sentences ask questions, they need a question mark at the end. Here are some questions that may be in our writing."

Who was there? ("This needs a question mark at the end.")

What time do I go? ("This needs a question mark at the end.")

Why did he do that? ("This needs a question mark at the end.")

Where are we going? ("This needs a question mark at the end.")

Putting an Exclamation Mark to Show Excitement

"When we want to show excitement, we put an exclamation mark at the end of the sentence we are excited about. Here are some sentences that we might want to end with exclamation marks."

I like New York City! ("This sentence shows some place I am excited about, so I will put an exclamation mark at the end of this sentence.")

The zoo was great! ("This sentence shows an exciting place I went, so I will put an exclamation mark at the end of this sentence.")

We have so much fun! ("This sentence shows something I am excited about, so I will put an exclamation mark at the end.")

Look out! ("I am excited here because I think something bad might happen, so I will put an exclamation mark at the end of this sentence.")

Mini-Lesson Focus: What to Do When You Are "Stuck" ("I ain't got nothing to write about!")

Some children always have something to tell the teacher and the class and have no trouble coming up with writing topics. Other children find it harder to think of topics to write about each day (or every few days when they add on and don't write about something new each day!). If teachers can get children thinking about the many things they do each day or the many things they know a lot about (sometimes more than the teacher!), writing is easier. Giving topics is not the solution! It causes new problems—problems for the children who know nothing about that topic. Writing is easy once the children know what they want to write about. In Four-Blocks classrooms, we stress that when you write, you write about what you want to tell. During their mini-lessons, we often think aloud about what we might want to "tell them today." As the children listen in on our thinking, they see how we decide what we want to tell them, and they get some ideas about what they might tell us. Here is what a mini-lesson might look and sound like when you have some kids that are "stuck:"

The teacher thinks aloud:

"Let's see...what do I want to tell you about today? I could tell you about my new 'teacher sweater' and where I got it. I could tell you about the basketball game I watched on T.V.— it was wonderful because my team won! I could tell you about the new family that moved into my neighborhood. Today, I want to write a story I thought of yesterday during Self-Selected Reading when Jason shared *Zoo-Looking* with me during our conference."

The teacher thinks aloud as she writes:

> One day a boy named Jason went to the circus.
> Jason looked at the elephants as they walked
> around the tent. The elephants didn't look back.
> Jason looked at acrobats as they swung from
> their swings. The acrobats didn't look back.
> Jason looked at the clowns as they did tricks.
> The clowns didn't look back. Jason looked at
> me, and I looked back.

The teacher tells about other favorite books the children might be inspired by:

"I thought of this story when Jason and I read *Zoo-Looking* yesterday. Can any of you think of books that might inspire you to write a similar book?"

Other Ideas for What to Do When You Are "Stuck"

Thinking Aloud about a Few Topics You Don't Write about

Think aloud about two or three topics you don't write about every time you start a new piece. Let the children know that just because you don't use those topics doesn't mean they can't!

"I could write about picking apples in the mountains. Or, I could write about my daughter's new video game. But I think I will write about my neighbor who hit my mailbox." Think out loud as you write about this.

> My neighbor rang my bell on Saturday. She was driving her new car and hit my mailbox! The mailbox was lying in the . . .

After you finish say, "Now many of you don't have a neighbor who hit your mailbox, but you have picked apples, grapes, peaches, or pecans. You could write about one time when you helped someone pick something. I know lots of you have games you have not written about. Someone might want to tell us about his favorite game.

Making a List of Topics to Write About

Make the list on the chalkboard or on a piece of paper. Let the children start their own lists inside their notebooks or writing folders.

Things to Write About

1. My friends
2. My favorite games
3. A good book
4. A favorite time with Grandpa (Grandma)
5. A visit to the barber (hairdresser)

Rereading the First Part of a Favorite Book (Don't Finish!), then, Writing Your Own Ending

Reread the beginning of *The Mitten* by Jan Brett. Get inspired! Change the mitten to a glove and have different animals decide on different fingers to live in!

> A little boy lost a glove. Along came a rabbit—into the ring finger he went. Along came a frog—into the thumb finger he went. Along came a . . .

Making a List of Places You Can Write About

Talk about the places you go to or would like to go to. Make a list of them one day. Choose a place on that list to write about another day.

Places I Could Write About

1. New York City
2. School
3. The Grocery Store

Mini-Lesson Focus: Adding to Editor's Checklist (Stays on Topic)

Add something else to your Editor's Checklist when the children have become very quick and automatic at reading the teacher's writing for these items and when they are in the habit of checking their own writing for the items. Staying on topic is often the last item added to a first-grade checklist. Some first-grade teachers can and do add more items to their lists. The children in your class should determine how many items are on the Editor's Checklist! Do not more add items than most of your children can self-edit for. Here is a mini-lesson to add "staying on topic" to the Editor's Checklist.

The teacher says:

"You are becoming such good editors that I think it is time to add one more item to our checklist. Most of you do this already. When we write, we try to write all about the topic we have chosen. Sometimes, writers include things they are interested in but that have nothing to do with the topic. This is another thing editors always look for when they are editing a piece. They look to see that everything the writer writes is about the topic." The teacher adds #7 to the checklist and says, "Number seven on our checklist is staying on topic."

Editor's Checklist

1. Name and date
2. Sentences make sense
3. Beginning capital letters
4. Ending punctuation (. ? !)
5. Circle misspelled words
6. Capital letters for names and places
7. Stays on topic

"Today, after I finish writing, you will edit my writing for all seven items on the list."

The teacher writes, leaving out one period and one capital for a name. She also stretches out and misspells two words and writes a short sentence that is not on topic.

Mrs. Cunningham   February 7

Abraham Lincoln

Abraham Lincoln lived long ago. He grew up in a log cabin. He liked to read and lern. (Stretches out and misspells **learn**.) He was a loyer (Stretches out and misspells **lawyer**, then forgets the period.) He was our sixteenth president. Do you remember all of the presidents? (This is the sentence that is not on topic.) Abraham lincoln (Lowercase letter for his last name.) freed the slaves. We remember him each year on Presidents' Day.

The teacher and the class edit the piece, adding the period and capital letter, circling **lern** and **loyer**, and crossing out the sentence about all the presidents.

Other Ideas for Adding to Editor's Checklist (Staying on Topic)

Using "Thumbs Up" and "Thumbs Down" to Determine If Each Sentence Stays on Topic

Continue to use your Editor's Checklist every day. Do not make lots of mistakes, but focus on the errors you see most often in your student's writing. This makes you aware of a need to be reinforced. The latest item added to the checklist is always a good choice. When deciding whether a sentence stays on topic, use an every-student-response signal: "Thumbs up if the sentence stays on topic, thumbs down if the sentence does not stay on the topic."

First Grade

We learn math. (thumbs up)
We write every day. (thumbs up)
We read every day. (thumbs up)
We all like pizza. (thumbs up)
Our teacher reads to us every day. (thumbs up)

Writing a Story and Adding a Sentence That Is Not on Topic

Write about someone in your class or something the children in your class like to do. Add a sentence that is not on topic. Read the piece as a class and do a thumbs up or thumbs down for each sentence staying on topic.

David Plays Basketball

David likes to play basketball. He is on the YMCA's basketball team. He plays in their basketball games. He is a good reader. In one game, David scored 10 points. He helped win the game!

Writing an Informational Piece and Adding a Sentence That Is Not on Topic

Write about something you are studying or the topic of an informational book you just read. Add a sentence that is not on topic. Read the piece as a class and do a thumbs up or thumbs down for each sentence that stays on the topic.

Wind

When air moves, we call this wind. Wind moves clouds. Wind makes trees move. Wind blows kites and clothes. The sun shines in the sky. Wind can be gentle or dangerous.

Writing about a Book You Read and Adding a Sentence That Does Not Belong

Write about a book you have read to your class or a story your class has read during Guided Reading. Add a sentence that is not on topic—did not happen in the book. Read the piece as a class and do a thumbs up or thumbs down for each sentence.

Mirandy and Brother Wind

The author of this story is Patricia McKissack. This story takes place in spring. It is about a cakewalk. We had one at our fall festival. Mirandy. . .

Mini-Lesson Focus: Writing an Informational Piece (Using a Web to Organize)

When teachers and first-graders think about writing, they often think about writing "stories." When we write about things we are learning about or things we know a lot about, they are not really "stories." We call them informational pieces. Informational texts are not structured in the same way that stories are. Writing informational pieces is different from writing stories. We focus on how to write an informational piece in this mini-lesson.

The teacher thinks aloud about what to write:

"Sometimes I write about things we are studying in first grade. Sometimes you write about the things you know a lot about—like snakes or dinosaurs. When people write about something, and they want to make sure they tell everything they know, they often start with a web. A web helps organize the information. If I chose to write about Martin Luther King, Jr., a web would help me organize everything I know about him. If I chose a dinosaur to write about, a web would help me organize what I know about that dinosaur. Today, since we are studying about birds, I am going make a web about birds and then use that web to write about birds."

The teacher starts a web, thinks aloud, and writes:

"Since I am going to write about birds, I will put that in the middle. I want to tell where they live, what they eat, the parts of a bird, and then tell about some local birds we have studied. So I will put those four things in ovals around the corners. (Makes the web as he talks.)

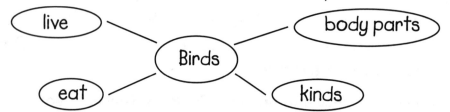

The teacher adds to the web, thinks aloud, and writes:

The teacher talks about the kinds of homes birds live in; especially those most familiar in his area (nests in trees) as she fills in that "spoke" of the web. He talks about the parts of a bird, which is the next "spoke" he might fill in. He remembers to mention that only birds have feathers. He talks about the third "spoke"—what birds eat. He might talk about what people feed birds. When he gets to the final "spoke," he adds the names of all the familiar birds first-graders in his area may see.

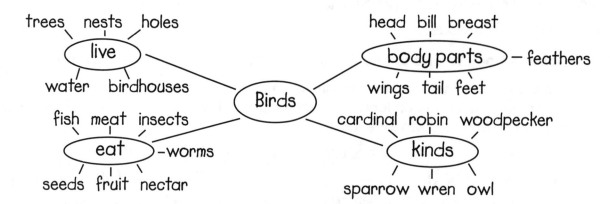

When the teacher finishes the web, he reads and reviews it with his children.

Other Ideas for Writing an Informational Piece

Using a Web to Write Informational Pieces

Use the web you created to structure an informational piece about birds. Show the children how to write a sentence about the topic. Then, include information from each spoke of the web to write the information in an organized way.

Birds

Each spring we see the birds return to our area. Some birds build nests in trees. Other birds live in a hole in a tree or a birdhouse. Birds eat seeds, worms, and insects. Birds have wings . . .

Using a Paragraph Frame to Write about What You Learned

A paragraph frame is another way to organize information and write. The teacher creates the frame. Each child writes a paragraph, finishing the sentences with the information that he or she chooses. Children who struggle to write often experience success with the structure of paragraph frames and are proud of their finished pieces.

Birds

I learned that birds live in _____. I learned that birds eat _____. Another thing I learned was _____. The most interesting thing I learned was _____.

Making a Web to Write about a Person's Life

Create a web about a person (Lincoln, Washington, Martin Luther King, Jr., or a professional or Olympic athlete). Use the web to write an informational piece, showing the children how to write a sentence about the topic and the, use each spoke of the web to write the information in an organized way.

Martin Luther King, Jr.

Martin Luther King, Jr. was born in Georgia. He grew up in a segregated world. (Stretch this out and write what you hear.) He became . . .

Making a Web about an Informational Book You Read (and writing from that Web)

After reading an informational book (about plants or any other topic you study in first grade), create a web. Then, write an informational piece showing the children how to write a sentence about the topic (plants) and how to use each spoke of the web to write the information in an organized way.

Plants

We are learning about plants. We learned how to plant seeds. Plants need sunshine, soil, and water to grow. Plants . . .

Later in First Grade–Getting Better

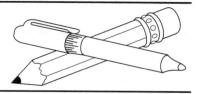

These last mini-lessons are mini-lessons you might want to do in the last month of school. Some first-grade classes will be ready for these and others won't. These lessons teach children how to revise and partner edit, both of which require a fairly high level of thinking and writing sophistication. Because many first-grade teachers like to have the children create some class books and duplicate these for everyone to take home, we also include three focused writing possibilities that many first-grade teachers have found success with late in the year.

For those teachers that feel their students have just begun to write, we suggest that you go back to some of the early lessons and do some of them "one more time." You will find students who were not ready to do the things you were modeling in the early lessons are ready later in the year. Look at the writing of the students in your class and ask yourself, "What aren't they doing that most first graders can do? How can I help them? What do many students need another lesson on?" The modeling, coaching, and praising at this time of year will go a long way for your late bloomers.

For those teachers who have a basal containing focused writing lessons, you may want to try a few of them at the end of the year now that your children can write. Consider doing some lessons the teacher's manual suggests as "class lessons" or "interactive writing" and write together with your children. Remember, you do not need to do a single lesson suggested in the basal to produce good writers in first grade—just ask Denise Boger! What is important is letting your first graders watch you think aloud and write. These activities will produce children who not only can write in first grade, but children who want to write each day.

Often schools or school systems have certain areas of writing teachers are asked to "cover" at different grade levels. We have left you some time to be able to do these lessons. But remember to model, model, model—don't just assign! One lesson we have not touched upon that many teachers do successfully in first grade is writing a letter. Some write letters at Christmas or Valentine's Day. *The Jolly Postman* by Janet and Allan Ahlberg is a wonderful way to introduce youngsters to letters and letter writing. Read the book during your teacher read-aloud and then write a letter during your mini-lesson. Your students may be able to think a lot of storybook characters they know to write to that the authors did not mention in their book! Writing to real people is another mini-lesson for another day. *Messages in the Mailbox* by Loreen Leedy is a book about how to write a letter. In this book children learn how to write a friendly letter, a thank-you letter, a fan letter, etc. Children also learn how to address an envelope. This may be a little advanced for some first graders, but not for others at this time of year! This is a wonderful book and activity just before a field trip to the post office! If you think your students are up to this, you might create a post office in your room and let your students write letters and notes to each other. Choose a letter to model each day for a week and watch your students begin to get the writing bug! The end of the year is always a good time to stretch your students. Just don't expect all first graders to write wonderful letters.

Other lessons we have not mentioned that first grade teachers sometimes model are Words in a Series Have Commas between Them and How to Use Quotation Marks When People Talk. These lessons are usually modeled and talked about by the teacher, but mastery of these skills is not expected by first grade students and the items are never put on the Editor's Checklist.

April is poetry month. Reading poetry by Shel Silverstein and other well-liked poets during Self-Selected Reading time can be followed by writing poetry for your mini-lesson. Most children at this age think that poetry has to rhyme and some are surprised to learn that this isn't true.

Don't be discouraged if your children aren't ready for these lessons in first grade. If most children can experience success with the self-selected writing and publishing described in the previous section, you have had a very good year, and your students are well on their way to becoming very good readers and writers. For those classes who are ready, however, these lessons are the "icing on the cake" of a powerful first-grade writing experience.

Mini-Lesson Focus: Modeling Revision Using Think-Alouds

First-grade teachers are usually comfortable editing with young children. They like to edit because they know what to do. Teachers easily find missing capital letters and fix the wrong punctuation marks at the end of sentences. Teachers can recognize misspelled words and can correct them. Most teachers are not as comfortable with revision. They often wonder how much you should ask young children to revise their writing and how much revision to teach to emergent writers. First-graders shouldn't be expected to do much revision, but most first-graders can learn to reread what they have written and think about how to make it better. As with all writing skills, the best way to teach revision is by modeling, modeling, modeling! Here is a mini-lesson that focuses on revision:

The teacher reads a piece she has chosen to publish and asks the children to help her make it clearer or more interesting:

Scarborough Beach

One of my favorite places to visit is Scarborough Beach. It is in Rhode Island. I go there once every year—sometimes more! I like to hear the ocean. I like to watch the men on boats, fishing in the ocean. I like to go to the wonderful restaurants to eat seafood. I like to shop at the little shops along the coast. I like to visit with family nearby.

The teacher asks the children some questions:

"Does my piece have a good beginning?"

"Is there anything you think I need to add?"

"Is everything in the right order?"

"Does it have a good ending?"

"Can you think of anything that would make this piece better or more interesting?"

The teacher thinks aloud about the children's responses and revises her piece:

If the children think it needs a better beginning (and the teacher agrees), then the teacher helps the class write a better introductory sentence. If the children want to know something ("How do you get there?"), she may add another sentence or two.

Sometimes I drive to Rhode Island. Sometimes I fly there.

Thinking about each question helps her look at the writing and offers a chance to "make it better" by adding or changing a word, changing the order of the sentences, or adding something to the end.

Scarborough Beach is a special place for me!

Other Ideas for Modeling Revision Using Think-Alouds

Teaching Children How to Revise by Starting with a Good Sentence

Many children have little trouble writing a good sentence at the beginning of their writing. For other children, this can be a problem! Good writing "hooks" the reader or listener from the start. Starting a story or an informational piece with a good (introductory) sentence is important. Look through your students' writing to find a good piece that does not start with a good sentence. Help the child change it in a class mini-lesson.

Snakes
A blacksnake will not hurt you.

This piece starts with a sentence about one kind of snake. Ask the writer why he chose to write about snakes. Use his answer to help come up with one or two new beginning sentence possibilities, such as:

Some people do not like snakes. I do! or I know a lot about snakes.

Teaching How to Revise by Adding . . . "Tell Me More!"

Remember the song from the musical and movie *Grease* that went something like this, "Tell me more, tell me more?" Some children start writing and stay on topic, but do not tell us enough. They need to tell us more. We can encourage them to "tell us more" by singing this little song to them! Do a mini-lesson on this using the writing of several children who are getting ready to publish. This is also a good technique to use when conferencing with individual children.

Teaching How to Revise by Putting Things in the Right Order or Sequence

Often young children tell the whole story, but don't tell it in the right order. They tell the events as they remember them. Helping children to put the events in the right sequence will make their writing easier to understand for those who read it.

Teaching How to Revise by Combining Sentences

Often writers have too many sentences and need to combine some. One child wrote:

My mother likes goldfish. My father likes goldfish. My sister likes goldfish.

The teacher suggested that he combine the sentences and write:

My mother, father, and sister like goldfish.

The child decided to write: My whole family likes goldfish.

Using Student's Writing to Teach Revision by Adding a Good Ending

One common problem young children have is to write a good story which just seems to stop without any real ending. Read one or two good stories that your young authors have chosen to publish which need good endings. Let the class make suggestions. Help them to see that some pieces just need a summary sentence:

What a good time I had with my Grandma that day.

Sometimes the writing just needs a closing sentence.

That is a dream I will never forget!

Mini-Lesson Focus: Self-Editing and Peer Editing

Most first-grade children can learn to self-edit. Once the teacher is editing with the class and the Editor's Checklist is growing, the teacher often gives the children their own Editor's Checklist to put inside their notebooks or writing folders. Each time a new item is added, the children get a new list. When children are finished writing a piece, they should "self-edit" using the checklist. Some first-grade children excel at self-editing while others are not capable of doing much better than they did on first draft without someone's help. As one first-grader (who hadn't done much editing) said, " I did the best I could!" We teach self-editing every time we let the children help edit our piece at the end of a mini-lesson. Late in first grade, we highlight peer editing by modeling it in several mini-lessons.

The teacher reads and thinks aloud about revising the piece she has chosen to publish:

My Cat Stormy

My cat Stormy was reskood from a storm drain. One night after a big thunderstorm, my cat was missing. A friend drove to work the next morning. He saw Stormy sitting there in the storm drain. Stormy was soking wet! My friend works at an office miles away. He picked up my wet cat. He brought Stormy home to me.

"Let's read my story together, and you can help me think about revising it." The class likes the beginning of the story and thinks the sentence, **My friend works at an office miles away** needs to be moved up. The teacher agrees and does this. The class wants a better ending and helps the teacher come up with: We were so happy to have him home. That is when we decided to change his name to stormy!

Next, the teacher chooses a child to be her partner and help her edit her writing.

The child takes a red marker and edits the teacher's writing using the checklist

"Number one: It has the name and date. I put the first check at the top."

"Number two: All the sentences make sense. A second check."

"Number three: Do all the sentences begin with a capital letter? Yes, another check."

"Number four: One of the sentences we added needs a period at the end." The editor adds this and then puts a check at the top.

"Number five: Are the misspelled words circled? Yes, the misspelled words are circled." The editor puts another check on top and since this will be published, the teacher writes the correct spelling of **rescued** and **soaking** above these words.

"Number six: The name **Stormy** in the last sentence needs a capital letter. The editor changes this and then puts a check at the top.

"Number seven: The sentences all stay on topic and a final check is put at the top.

Other Ideas for Self-Editing and Peer Editing

Continuing to Do a "Quick Edit" of the Teacher's Writing as Each Piece Is Written

Often when visitors come to Four-Blocks first-grade classrooms, they are shocked to see how well most of the children write and self-edit their pieces. Many children automatically include ending punctuation and beginning capitals on all their sentences (or at least on all the sentences they realize are sentences!). People and place names almost always have capital letters. When children finish writing, they automatically reread each sentence, referring to the checklist and fixing a few things they notice need fixing. "How do you get this to happen?" the visitors regularly ask. The answer is simple, yet crucial. From the time the teacher begins an Editor's Checklist, she leads the children to use the checklist to edit her writing every time she finishes a piece. When the teacher is writing pieces that she finishes in one day, the piece is quick-edited that day. The daily practice of doing this is the "magic potion" that produces so many able and confident writers by the end of first grade.

Editing Mini-Lesson

When the teacher is writing longer pieces that take several days to write, the piece takes longer to edit. For longer pieces, the teacher usually takes the entire mini-lesson time one day when the piece is finished to let the children edit her piece. Children love to be the teacher's editor and find and fix her mistakes.

Doing a Class Editing of a Student's Writing

Let a child who is getting ready to publish revise the piece with the class's help. Then, let the class use the checklist to edit the child's piece just as they edit the teacher's piece.

Doing Lots of Lessons in which You Choose Someone to Be Your Editing Partner

Children love being given the red marker and being the teacher's editing partner. Choose some of your "natural editors" to do this job as everyone watches. Be sure to express your appreciation for their help in making your piece so much more readable.

Partnering your Students and Letting Them Edit Each Other's Writing

Put your children in pairs, and let them edit each other's writing. Partner children of similar writing ability. This is not something to do in most first-grades until late in the year, but when the children have seen lots of helpful modeling, they are usually eager to be "wonderful editors!"

Mini-Lesson Focus: Revision by Finding a Better Word

Good writing can often be made much better by changing a few words. This is a revision step. Some first-grade children really enjoy doing this; other children don't. Children who like "words" like trying to find better words. Another reason to teach first-grade children to find a better word is that they often use the same words over and over again in their writing. Two examples of this are writing that something is "nice" or "good." Modeling "finding a better word" is an easy mini-lesson and children who are ready for this skill will pick it up easily. After the mini-lesson, you will find some children doing this revision as they read their writing to you.

The teacher thinks aloud and tells the class:

"Sometimes when I am reading over my story to make sure it makes sense, I see that I have used the same word over and over, or I might read a sentence and think of a better word to use in that sentence. I just cross out the word that I've decided not to use and write in the better word above it."

The teacher reads a piece she has written on a previous day:

The Grocery Store

Our class went on a field trip to Lowe's Foods. It is a grocery store near school. We walked there. The manager showed us around the store. We saw produce. We saw meats. We saw the rows of cans and boxes of food. We saw dairy products. We saw the bakery. They gave us all a cookie. The cookie was good. We learned a lot at the grocery store.

The teacher thinks aloud and models this process, crossing out some words, and writing words she thinks will make the writing better.

The Grocery Store

Our class went on a field trip to Lowe's Foods. It is a grocery store near our school. We walked there. The manager showed us around the store. We saw ~~produce~~ fruits and vegetables. ~~We saw meats.~~ Next, we went to the meat department. We ~~saw~~ walked down the ~~rows~~ aisles of cans and boxes of food. We saw ~~dairy products~~ milk, cheese, and butter. ~~We saw the~~ They had a bakery with cakes, pies, doughnuts, and cookies. They gave us all a cookie. The cookie was ~~good~~ delicious. We learned a lot at the grocery store.

Writing Mini-Lessons for First Grade: The Four-Blocks® Model © Carson-Dellosa CD-2417

Other Ideas for Revision by Finding a Better Word

Ending Those "Love Stories"

Some children have been writing those "love stories" for a long time. (In November: *My Family*. I love my dad. I love my mom. I love my. . . . In January: *Winter* I love snow. I love making snowmen. I love going ice skating. I love. . . . In March: *St. Patrick's Day* I love green, etc.) Using a pattern helps some children write, but after doing this for a while, it is time for children to move on. The best way to make children aware of this and help them change is to do a mini-lesson on it.

St. Patrick's Day

I like St. Patrick's Day. Everyone wears green. We hear about leprechauns. Leprechaun are little, green. . .

Finding a Better Word for an Overused Word ("Said")

Another mini-lesson you can do in first grade is to brainstorm words that you might use in place of overused words. An example of this would be to brainstorm better words for "said," such as called, shouted, exclaimed, cried, yelled, whispered, groaned, whined, etc. Then, start writing and use these suggestions.

The boy shouted to his dog, "Here, Prince, come here!" When Joey got home found lunch was not ready yet. "Oh, no," whined Joey. Then, he whispered to his dog, "Let's . . .

Describing What You Mean by "Nice"

Write about someone. Describe the person physically (height, hair color, etc.) then say that he is "nice". Read your writing over and decide that the class does not know what "nice" means. Cross out nice and tell how the person is nice.

He is nice. Change the sentence:

He is always polite. He says, "Please" and "Thank you."

Describing What You Mean by "Good"

Write about something. Describe a picnic lunch and say that it was "good." Read your writing over and decide that the class does not know what "good" means. Cross out good and be more specific.

It was good. Change the sentence:

The sandwiches were delicious. We also had potato chips, apples, and chocolate chip cookies.

Reminding Students in Author's Chair

This is something that you can also remind your students of when they are reading their writing in the Author's Chair. A question to model asking your students is, "Could you tell us more about _____?"

Mini-Lesson Focus: Writing Is Like Juggling

Writing, like reading, is a complex cognitive process. Children have many things to remember, or "juggle," when writing. Children must think of a topic that they want to tell about and what exactly they want to tell, capital letters, ending punctuation, good handwriting, how to spell many words, and how to stretch out other words and write the letters that represent the sounds they hear. Teachers who are most successful at teaching writing look at what their children are doing and let the children's daily writing tells them what they need to teach. We can't cover everything a child needs to know about writing every day. Occasionally, however, we do a lesson in which we think aloud about all the "balls writers must juggle."

The teacher thinks aloud and writes:

Choosing a Topic

"I could write about my best friend. We all have good friends that we like to write about. I could write about all the flowers I planted in my backyard yesterday after school. I thought since we were planting flowers at school, I should plant some at home. But, I think I will write about Junie B. Jones, the girl in the chapter book I am reading to you. You all like her so much, I thought that would be a good topic."

Deciding What to Write about the Book—or Narrowing the Topic

"I could write a summary of the story with a beginning, middle, and end. I could tell you why I like this book. I really like the main character. I could write all about the main character, Junie B. Jones, and I think I will!"

Writing a Good Sentence Using Capital Letters, Spelling, and Periods at the End

"My first sentence is Junie B. Jones is in kindergarten. Junie B. Jones has three capitals in her name. I know how to spell her name by looking at the cover of the book. I know how to spell **is** and **in** because they are on the word wall and have been up most of the year. Kindergarten is not on the Word Wall or in the room, so I will stretch that word out and write the sounds I hear kin-der-gar-den. I remember to put my period at the end."

Staying on Topic, Capital Letters at the Beginning of Sentences, Ending Punctuation, and Spelling

"My next sentence tells why I like Junie B. Jones."

She says the funniest things.

"I begin with a capital letter because sentences begin with capital letters. I know how to spell **she**. **Say** is on the word wall, so I add an **s** for **says**. **The** is another Word Wall word. **Funny** is on the Word Wall, but I have to change the **y** to **i** and add **est** like we do on the back of our Word Wall paper. **Things** is on the Word Wall, too. (By the end of the year, many words the children need are there!).

The teacher continues writing and thinking aloud as she writes.

Most days, the mini-lesson focuses on one point. This mini-lesson reminds children of all the thinking writers do. Writing *is* really like juggling!

Other Ideas for Writing Is Like Juggling

Modeling What to Do When You're "Stuck"

All writers occasionally have trouble thinking of something to write about. (Even teachers have that problem!) The children need to know that all writers and authors get "writer's block" when they are not sure what to write about next. A writer or author might take a break when this happens but would never just stop writing. Look at your list of "Topics We Could Write About" on the wall or in your writing notebook or folder. Another idea is to look around the room to get ideas. Model this for the students. For example, the teacher might look up at a stuffed animal and be reminded of a "story" about a stuffed animal that comes to life. The teacher might look at some crayons and be reminded of the time "I used my crayons to draw a picture for my brother on his wall!" Then, write and model everything writers have to remember.

Getting Your Thoughts on Paper—Students Can Help

Sometimes you know what to write about, but have trouble getting your thoughts on paper. Model this for your students and ask them to help you. I went to watch Chip and Chad play T-Ball last night. I want to write about it, but I don't know much about the game. Will those of you who know all about T-Ball help me? This is the perfect time for the children to do a shared or interactive writing mini-lesson. Remind the students of all the things they need to know, besides knowing how to play T-Ball, to help you write this story.

Juggling Spelling—So Many Things to Remember

By the fourth quarter of the year, most first-grade classrooms have about 100 words on the Word Wall. Daily Word Wall practice and review helps everyone know which words are on the wall and where the words are. Children do need to be reminded, however, to refer to the Word Wall, theme boards, and charts in the room and use them! They also need to hear us model other ways to spell words that we practice during Working with Words—adding **s** to nouns for plurals and to make verbs sound right, adding **-er** and **-est** to words, and changing beginning letters to spell new words that rhyme with Word Wall words. Most first-graders need constant modeling of how we stretch out words and write the sounds that represent those letters. Mini-lessons on the different ways we spell words as we write need to be continued throughout the first-grade year.

Juggling Grammar

We introduce writing to children by explaining to them that writing is "telling." As the year goes on, however, we want children to learn that sometimes we don't write things exactly the way we say them. Many children say, "My friend and me went to the mall." Asking children, "Does that sound right?" doesn't help. One little first-grader responded, "Sounds right to me!" and he was right, it did sound right to him. That was just the way he and his friends said it. If writing is like telling, we need to let them write as they talk—except when we are "making it public." If the student is not publishing, we do not correct grammar. When a piece is being published, however, we correct grammar by simply saying, "That is a way to say it. But when we write it, we write it this way." Later in first grade, many teachers do mini-lessons in which they correct the grammar in a piece that is about to be published by making the "way we say it—way we write it" distinction.

Mini-Lesson Focus: Focused Writing of Stories

Most first-graders write about things they know in their "all about" stories. First-grade children write all about their friends, all about their pets, all about their trips, etc. They tell "real" stories instead of making up stories and writing "fiction." First-graders don't usually write stories with a beginning, middle, and end unless we model this for them. Later in the year when most of the students are writing well (for first-graders!), teachers often do a focused writing lesson on "stories." They model writing a story for the mini-lesson, and then the children write stories. Here is an example focused on a special day in first grade.

The teacher tells what she will write about and then writes her story:

" We have had many good days in first grade. I remember the first day when we were all new to each other and the days when new students came to our class. I remember lots of birthdays—even the day I told you it was my birthday! I remember the fall festival, our Thanksgiving feast, our Valentine's Day party, and all the days we had visitors. I remember the assemblies we have watched and the books we have read. Today, I am going to tell you a story about one special day in first grade. This is a true story; it really did happen. My story about a special day in first grade will have a beginning, middle, and end. Watch and see what I have chosen to write about."

First Grade

She writes the beginning.

I remember the first day of first grade. I didn't know you and you didn't know me. We learned each other's names quickly. We started the day with a class meeting.

The teacher has the children read the beginning with her, discusses it, and then writes the middle.

I read a favorite book to you. I talked about the different ways first-graders can read books. Then, I let you look at the baskets of books on your tables. We drew a picture of ourselves and told about ourselves. We talked about the different books we would read in Guided Reading, and we read a big book together. At math time, we graphed how we got to school. We all had lunch in the cafeteria.

The teacher has the children read the middle with her, discusses it, and then writes the end.

After lunch, we talked about the themes we would study in first grade. Then we toured the school and played outside. The last thing I did was write about the day.

"We have had many good days together since then. That is what I want you to write about today—a special day you remember in first grade. When we finish these stories, we will edit and publish them, and put them in a class book. I will make copies of the book for everyone to take home so you can remember your friends and first grade, and your parents can see how well you are writing."

The teacher discusses what day each child might like to write about as he dismisses them one by one to go back to their seats and write.

He starts with children who already know what they will write about and have their hands raised and happy, confident looks on their face.

"What day are you going to write about, Suzanne?" ("My birthday when I brought cupcakes for every-one.") "Ryan?" ("My first day at Clemmons. I was scared!") "DaSawndra?" ("The day I made my first book.") The teacher continues like this so that he knows every child has something to write about, and their topics are not all the same. If a child does not have an idea, the teacher helps him come up with one.

Most children need several days to write the stories while the teacher circulates, encourages, and helps. Next, the stories need to be self-edited and peer-edited, and then edited by the "chief editor," the teacher! Then, the stories need to be typed on the computer (perhaps by a parent volunteer). Finally, the stories need to be published by duplicating them for the whole class and binding them together to create a class book.

What do the children do if they finish their story before the other children? Return to self-selected topics!

Other Ideas for Focused Writing of Stories

Teaching How to Write Fiction

Young children like tell their stories, but making up a story is harder. Some children do make up stories. These children are usually familiar with how stories are written because someone has read to them since they were very young. First-grade teachers need to model fiction by "making up a story" and writing this in a mini-lesson.

"I think about how many of the stories we read are written. Sometime they begin, 'Once upon a time' or 'In a far away place,' or just tell where the story takes place or what it was like. I will begin that way."

In a little village far, far away lived a boy named David and a dinosaur. The boy wanted . . .

Writing Team Stories

Divide the class into teams or groups. Give each team or group time to write the beginning of a story together. Have them edit it because another team will read it the next day. Make sure the stories are readable before the next day. The next day, each team reads the beginning of another team's story and adds a middle. On the third day, each group gets a story they haven't seen before and adds an ending. You may need to assign the "writer" who will do the actual writing for each group. This should be someone who can write quickly and legibly so everyone can read it.

Mini-Lesson Focus: Focused Writing of an Informational Class Book

Later in the year, first-grade teachers often do some focused writing lessons related to the science or social studies topics being studied. Children write and illustrate their pieces and this writing is compiled in a class book. The book is added to the material available for Self-Selected Reading. Children love reading class books. A focused writing lesson often takes a week or more from start to finished book. Here is an example from a class doing a study of birds in the spring of the year.

Day One

The teacher thinks aloud, the class brainstorms, and the teacher writes.

The teacher tells the class they are going to take a week off from their individual writing to make a class book about birds. They have been studying birds, and together they brainstorm the names of birds.

robin	bluebird	blue jay	sparrow	wren	gull
owl	woodpecker	cardinal	hummingbird	kiwi	hawk
crow	pigeon	flamingo	dove	oriole	ostrich
eagle	partridge	roadrunner	loon	chickadee	penguin
pelican	nightingale	creeper	goose	pheasant	
parrot	parakeet	turkey	duck	chicken	

The children work in groups to come up with questions about birds.

The children are put into groups of three or four, with a recorder in each group. Each group lists questions they should try to answer in their bird reports.

"What do they eat?"
"Where do they live?"
"What kind of nests do they live in?"
"What do the males look like?"
"What do the females look like?"
"How big are they?"
"What are their body parts?"
"What is an interesting fact about this bird?"

The children choose a bird to research and write about.

The teacher tells the children that each one of them will become an expert on one bird and write about it. Because she knows some birds will be more popular than others, she asks each child to list five birds they would like to write about. She then assigns each child a bird, assigning more familiar birds to less able writers. The teacher chooses a bird no one has chosen—the ostrich.

Day Two

The teacher models writing some facts she already knows about her bird, the ostrich.

Ostriches

very big   long necks

hide their heads in the sand

Each child writes some facts they already know about their bird.

The children begin researching birds.

They use books, magazines, encyclopedias, Web sites and whatever resources are available in the classroom and library. They take notes on big index cards.

Day Three

The children continue researching and writing facts. The teacher circulates and gives support to those who need it.

Day Four:

The teacher thinks aloud and models writing her report:

Ostriches

Ostriches are the fastest birds on land. They are . . . .

The children begin writing their reports, with help from the teacher as needed.

Days Five, Six, and Seven:

The children continue writing and partner edit their reports using the Editor's Checklist. The teacher does a final edit with each child. The reports are copied or typed and illustrated and put together into a class book.

Other Ideas for Focused Writing of an Informational Class Book

Writing about Social Studies Themes

One first-grade teacher did a month-long social studies unit on France. During this time, she encouraged the children to write about France and what they were learning. When the month was over, all but three children had done this! The teacher then sat down with each one of them and helped those three put on paper what they had learned.

Many of the teacher's mini-lessons during that month were related to France.

Paris

Paris is the largest city in France. It is famous for fashions, museums, and food. The Eiffel Tower is . . .

Writing about Summer

As the school year ends, some children are excited about summer vacation (and some teachers, too!). Capture the enthusiasm for summer and let the children tell you and their classmates about what they will do during this time. This is a class book that most children are really excited about making.

Mini-Lesson Focus: Focused Writing of a "How To" Class Book

Young children like to tell about how to make things. (Sometimes these stories make the local newspaper because their directions are very entertaining!) Teaching mini-lessons on writing directions help children focus on ordering events. In this lesson, children make a peanut butter and jelly sandwich for snack time. After making and enjoying their sandwich, the teacher and class compose directions for making a peanut butter and jelly sandwich. The following day, children work alone or in pairs to write recipes for favorite sandwiches.

The teacher thinks aloud about what to write:

"We have just finished making and eating peanut butter and jelly sandwiches, so now let's write about this. What did we do first? Yes, we get two pieces of bread."

Peanut Butter and Jelly Sandwich

First, we get two pieces of bread.

Next, we put peanut butter on one slice of bread.

Then, we put jelly on the other slice.

Finally, we put the two slices together and cut it in half.

Then, the best part comes. We get to eat it!

Talk about other sandwiches they make or someone makes for them.

"Tuna fish is one of my favorite sandwiches. My daughter's favorite is a grilled cheese. My wife likes a ham sandwich with tomatoes and mayonnaise on it. What is your favorite?"

Let the children tell about their favorite sandwiches and how they make them. Record their list.

tuna fish	tomato	bologna and cheese
egg salad	ham	banana and peanut butter
fried egg	grilled cheese	peanut butter and marshmallow
bologna	BLT	

On the following day, have children write down the directions for making their favorite sandwiches. Let children who like the same kind of sandwich write together.

The teacher edits, illustrates, and compiles these recipes. He duplicates a sandwich cookbook for each child to take home.

Other Ideas for Focused Writing of a "How To" Class Book

Doing a Science Experiment and Having the Children Write about What They Did

In Four-Blocks classrooms we try to integrate as much as possible. We like to tie our writing to the things we are learning in social studies and science.

"Yesterday, we planted seeds that will grow into plants. (They may be our Mother's Day presents!)"

Planting

Yesterday we planted seeds. First, we put dirt in a paper cup. Next, we poked three holes in the dirt. Then, we put the seeds into those holes. Finally we watered the seeds and put our cups in the sunshine of the windows. We will watch the seeds grow into marigolds!

Writing about Cooking (Cake, Cookies, Brownies, Turkeys, Favorite Dishes, etc.)

Talk about the many things you can cook. Think aloud about how you prepare these foods and cook them. Modeling one lesson about cooking usually leads to the famous "how to" stories that the children write by themselves; how to make a cake, cookies, gingerbread, etc. Children also like to write about baking a turkey, ham, or other favorite dish. This would make a wonderful cookbook for Mother's Day if you (or they) type the recipes and copy them to make cookbooks for all the children.

"I have a new recipe that I like and my daughter loves. It is Key Lime Pie. . .

Key Lime Pie

First you prepare a graham cracker crust (or buy one).

Next, you make the filling . . .

Writing about How to Play a Favorite Game

Talk about your favorite outside (soccer) or inside (Monopoly®) game. Write about that game.

Soccer

Soccer seems to be the rage. Everyone likes to play soccer lately. I like to watch soccer games, especially when I know the children playing on the teams. This is how you play soccer. . .

Have the children tell about their favorite games and how they play them.

Writing about How to Draw a Person (Face, House, Animal, etc.)

Combine art and writing. Draw a picture of a person's face, and write about how you do this. Have the children draw a picture and write about how they drew this object.

Mini-Lesson Focus: Young Authors' Conference

The focus of a good writing program in first grade is on children as authors. Setting aside time for children to share their writing is an important part of the writing process. It also gives students the opportunity to develop listening and speaking skills. After writing each day, the children get to share their writing with the other students in an Author's Chair format. This is a time when some children get ideas for stories they, too, can write. ("I have a bike in my garage. I can write about riding *my* bike." "I went to the lake fishing with my friend Jimmy. I could write about that." "I got a neat game for *my* birthday. I could tell about that.)

Publishing is an important part of daily writing, even in first grade. When publishing, children find a real reason to look at their writing to revise ("make it better"), edit ("make it right"), and publish ("make it public"). When you do not try to take every piece the children write to final copy, publishing is a more reasonable process.

We can let children have an even a wider audience at a "Young Authors' Conference". The last month of school is a good time for students to do this. If your students have been making books throughout the year, they can simply choose one of their books, read it to see if they can make it better (draw the pictures better, find a "typo" or a place where they did not recopy the editing correctly, make a newer, nicer cover, etc.).

If you have not been publishing, but your students have been writing in notebooks, folders, or you have been saving some writing on computer disks, then you already have the pieces that will become your books. If you have a computer, decide how you can get these stories written on the word processor. But, if they are written in the children's best handwriting, that is fine, too! Tell the class about the upcoming Young Authors' Conference and about the books they will share with family and friends.

Getting ready for a "Young Authors' Conference" will take some time, so plan ahead.

The teacher thinks aloud:

"These are some books (pieces) that I have written. Let me read them and see which one I like the best, or which one I think other people might like."

The teacher reads two or three of his books.

Since he doesn't have the number of published books the children in his class have (most teachers do not!) the teacher reads two or three pieces of writing. He talks about what he likes about each piece, and what he thinks other people would like about it. "I think people might like my piece about camel riding. I like my Abraham Lincoln piece. I did a good job telling about his life. My favorite is Scarborough Beach, but I do not think that would be everyone's favorite. I think I would like to make my piece about Abraham Lincoln and his life into my book for our Young Authors' Conference."

Next, the teacher goes through the publishing steps in the mini-lesson on pages 44 and 45.

He chooses a book to put the writing in. (Many teachers have parents help bind enough books for all the children in the class to use for the Young Authors' Conference, and then put the children's writing into these blank books. Other teachers have parents "bind" the books after the children finish with them.) In each book the teacher includes: the back and front cover, a title page, a dedication page, five to ten pages for the student's writing, and an "About the Author" page.

Other Ideas for Young Authors' Celebrations

Writing Invitations to the Young Authors' Conference or Tea

Tell the students about invitations and have them help you write a class invitation to the "Young Authors' Conference." Let the students copy this for their handwriting lesson and then take the invitations home to their family members.

You are invited to our Young Authors' Tea

Who: Family and Friends
When: May 12, 2003 at 2:00 P.M.
Where: Room 33, Clemmons Elementary
We hope you can come!

Writing about What Will Happen at the Young Authors' Conference or Tea

Talk about that day and what will happen. Children need to know what will happen at their "Young Authors' Conference" and what they are expected to do. By doing this mini-lesson, you will prepare your children for the events.

The Young Authors' Conference

First, we will divide into three groups. Each group has their special place in the room. Then, we will read our books to our parents, family members, and friends. Finally, we will have a tea. We will drink punch. We will eat cookies. It will be fun!

Writing about How Your Class Will Read Their Books

Think aloud, tell, and write about how your class will read their books.

We will divide into three groups to read our books. That way everyone can read, and it will not take all day! When it is your turn, you stand and read in a voice everyone can hear. Remember to practice reading so you will do a good job. You can clap after each book (or at the end—you decide!).

Having Young Authors Share with Other First-Grade Classes

Some teachers feel that a big celebration is not what they want, but they want to share their student's writing beyond the classroom. Sharing with the other first-grade classes is one way to do this. How many first grades? Each teacher divides the students in their class by that number. Three classes to divide by means the classes in thirds, and each teacher has a "sharing" time with $1/3$ of each class.

Having Young Authors Share with Older (or Younger) Children

Send your students to another, older grade level to read their writing. For example, pair with the fourth-grade teachers and send one third (if there are three classes) of your students, with their books, to each of the classrooms.

References

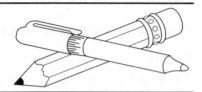

Professional References

Calkins, L. M. (1994) *The Art of Teaching Writing.* Portsmouth, NH: Heinemann Publishing.

Cunningham, P. M. and Hall, D. P. (1997) *Month-by-Month Phonics for First Grade.* Greensboro, NC: Carson-Dellosa Publishing, Co.

Cunningham, P. M.; Hall, D. P.; and Cunningham, J. W. (2000) *Guided Reading the Four-Blocks® Way.* Greensboro, NC: Carson-Dellosa Publishing, Co.

Cunningham, P. M.; Hall, D. P.; and Gambrell, L. B. (2002) *Self-Selected Reading the Four-Blocks® Way.* Greensboro, NC: Carson-Dellosa Publishing, Co.

Cunningham, P. M.; Hall, D. P.; and Sigmon, C. M. (1998) *The Teacher's Guide to the Four-Blocks®.* Greensboro, NC: Carson-Dellosa Publishing, Co.

Children's Books Cited

Alexander and the Terrible, Horrible, No Good, Very Bad Day by Judith Viorst (Atheneum, 1972).

Are You My Mother? by P. D. Eastman (Random House, 1988).

The Doorbell Rang by Pat Hutchins (Greenwillow, 1986).

Dr. Seuss's ABC: An Amazing Alphabet Book by Dr. Seuss (Random House, 1996).

Ira Sleeps Over by Bernard Waber (Houghton Mifflin Co., 1973).

The Jolly Postman or Other People's Mail by Janet and Allan Ahlberg (Little, Brown and Co., 2001).

Messages in the Mailbox: How to Write a Letter by Loreen Leedy (Holiday House, 1994).

Mirandy and Brother Wind by Patricia McKissack (Econo-Clad Books, 1999).

The Mitten by Jan Brett (Putnam Publishing Group, 1996).

The Relatives Came by Cynthia Rylant (Aladdin Books, 1985).

Robert the Rose Horse by Joan Heilbroner (Random House, 1989).

Stellaluna by Janelle Cannon (Scholastic, 1993).

There's an Alligator under My Bed by Mercer Mayer (E.P. Dutton, 1992).

There's a Nightmare in My Closet by Mercer Mayer (E.P. Dutton, 1987).

Zoo-Looking by Mem Fox (Mondo, 1996).

Notes

Notes

Notes

Notes

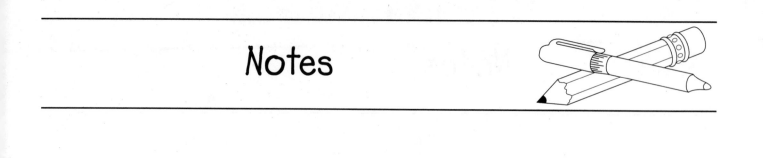